AWS

*A complete guide for beginners and
advanced users for amazon web services*

John C. Evans

CONTENTS

AMAZON WEB SERVICES (AWS)

Amazon Web Services (AWS) is a comprehensive cloud computing platform provided by Amazon. The first AWS offerings were launched in 2006 to offer online services for websites and client-side applications. The service is now available in 190 countries worldwide.

To minimize the impact of downtime and ensure the stability of the system, AWS is divided into regions with different data centers. These regions have central hubs in North America (region USA: East and West), South America (region Sao Paulo, Brazil), Europe / Middle East / Africa (region EU: Ireland, Frankfurt), and Asia Pacific (region the Asia Pacific and China).

The AWS portfolio includes over three dozen different web services, including:

Amazon Cloud Drive allows users to upload and access music, videos, documents, and photos from devices that are connected to the Internet. The service allows users to stream music and video on their devices.

Amazon CloudSearch is a scalable search service that is typically used to integrate customer-specific search functions into applications.

Amazon Dynamo Database (also DynamoDB or DDB) is a fully managed NoSQL database service that offers low latency and high scalability.

Amazon Elastic Compute Cloud 2 (EC2) is a web service that allows business customers to run applications on the scalable computing capacity. EC2 practically serves as an unlimited number of virtual machines (VM).

Amazon ElastiCache offers a fully managed caching service that is protocol compatible with Memcached, an open-source caching system for accelerating dynamic applications by reducing database load. ElastiCache also offers the open-source in-memory database Redis, which supports sorted data records and lists.

Amazon Mechanical Turk is a service for developers to access human intelligence resource when building their applications. The APIs allow human intelligence to be integrated into so-called remote procedure calls (RPCs) by using a network of people for tasks for which computers are ill-suited.

Amazon Redshift is a data warehouse service in the petabyte range that is designed for analytical workloads in conjunction with standard SQL clients and business intelligence (BI) tools.

Amazon Simple Storage Service (S3) is a scalable storage that can be used to store and access any amount of data. The service is used to secure and archive data and applications.

WHAT CAN AMAZON
WEB SERVICES DO?

What makes AWS so successful? Obviously, there are permanent innovations - since 2006, Amazon has been offering new services and features. The most recent major innovation in October of last year was the cooperation with VMware, from which the " VMware Cloud on AWS " emerged. Users can use it to supplement their conventional "on-premise" IT and the private cloud with resources from the public cloud - the classic hybrid cloud scenario.

The start was just as a classic in 2006, namely with infrastructure from the cloud. The target group for AWS was always different companies, never private users. The customers and partners of AWS took care of that, Dropbox would be mentioned here as an example, but other consumer offerings such as Netflix, Foursquare, or Reddit also rely on Amazon resources. Customers and partners can use many distributed data centers around the world.

Overview of important AWS services

The first service that AWS offered in 2006 was the Amazon Elastic Compute Cloud (Amazon EC2). It is a classic virtual server that runs either a Linux or a Windows server operating system. The offer is primarily aimed at developers. They do not have to enter into a fixed contract term and only pay for what they have actually used.

Other services soon followed. Amazon S3 (Simple Storage Service) offers highly scalable storage resources on demand. There are three storage classes: Amazon S3 Standard for the general storage of data with frequent access, Amazon S3 Standard - Infrequent Access (standard IA) for long-term data with less frequent access, and Amazon Glacier for long-term archiving.

Amazon CloudFront is a global content delivery network service designed to accelerate the delivery of websites, APIs, video content, and other web assets. The service can be integrated with other Amazon Web Services products and offers developers and companies the opportunity to provide content easily and without a minimum usage requirement.

Amazon, SimpleDB is a relational NoSQL database to outsource the workload for database administration. With Amazon SimpleDB, developers can store and query data items through web service requests.

Even Amazon DynamoDB is supported by fast, flexible NoSQL database service that both document and key-value store models. The service is designed for mobile, web, games, advertising, and IoT applications.

AWS Elastic Beanstalk is a service for deploying and scaling web applications and services developed with Java, .NET, PHP, Node.js, Python, Ruby, Go, and Docker on servers such as Apache, Nginx, Passenger, and IIS.

The directory service for the administration of users and resources AWS Identity and Access Management (IAM) allows the control of customer access to AWS services and resources. Different groups can be created, and access rights can be assigned.

Amazon CloudWatch is a monitoring service for AWS cloud resources and the apps that customers run on AWS. Metrics can be captured and tracked, log files can be collected and monitored, alarms can be set, and services can be installed automatically. CloudWatch monitors AWS resources such as instances of EC2, Amazon DynamoDB tables, and Amazon RDS DB.

Basically, Amazon Web Services offer a range of cloud-based services for

- data processing
- Storage
- databases
- analyzes
- networks
- mobile devices
- developer Tools
- Management tools
- or the Internet of Things (IoT).

They are used for web and mobile applications, game development, data processing, and data warehousing, as well as for storage, archiving, and much more. Here is an overview of what is now a very broad cloud offering. AWS developers are said to have been encouraged to come up with at least 1,000 new offers each year.

New fields of activity

Since the AWS re Invent 2016 customer conference, the topic of hybrid cloud has been at the top of the AWS agenda. No wonder: analysts predict enormous growth rates for the hybrid cloud. It can be used in a well-coordinated, interoperable configuration to take advantage of different cloud delivery models - from private clouds, mostly on-premise, to external clouds, mostly public.

The most common variant is to add additional external computing and storage resources to the existing environment. AWS took a step in this direction last October with the announcement of VMware Cloud on AWS. The deployment is scheduled for mid-2017.

In addition to the alliance with VMware, a cooperation with the specialist for cloud-based business applications Workday was also agreed at re Invent 2016. However, it is only one of many close collaborations that Amazon has agreed on over the past ten years. Here are the numerous innovations that AWS announced at its customer conference at the end of 2016.

Artificial intelligence

Of course, the AWS cannot avoid the hype topic of artificial intelligence or artificial intelligence (AI). The Amazon approach provides developers with opportunities for deep learning so that they can enrich their applications with it. The result would be self-learning apps.

Artificial intelligence works in principle like a human: There are 100 billion neurons in the brain that communicate with each other via synapses. As soon as a person trains something, the frequency of the impulses at the synapses increases - a pattern emerges. With so-called long-term potentiation (LTP), people memorize things. The intensity, the timing, and the number of impulses are decisive for success. The stronger the impulse, the more likely people will remember something. This is also how artificial neural networks work.

With " Alexa," Amazon has created an artificial neural network as a counterpart to the AI pioneer " Watson " from IBM. The development has consumed well over $ 100 million, according to Amazon, and is far from over.

The on-board computer of the Enterprise spaceship served as a model for Alexa.

Alexa's voice functions are currently being used in Amazon Echo - a product that has been heavily criticized by data protection experts. Nonetheless, the Echo and its close relative " Echo Dot " provide an outlook on what Amazon intends to do with its artificial intelligence: a little helper who can answer questions and initiate services when called.

The AWS recently announced the following additional AI functions:

Amazon Lex is a voice and text conversation interface building service. The learning engine that drives Alexa is now available to all developers.

Amazon Polly is a service that converts text to natural language. It supports 24 languages and 47 natural voices.

Amazon Rekognition offers a simple image analysis that should also recognize faces in images.

MXNet is a programmable open-source framework for deep learning applications that supports various artificial neural networks such as Convolutional Neural

Networks (CNN) and Long Short-Term Memory Networks (LSTM).

Amazon Machine Learning has been around for a long time and forms the basis for virtually all other "intelligent" services. In general, the development of AI is just beginning. Many large IT companies are currently developing corresponding products and services.

Looking for new revenue generators

As is known, Amazon's management is constantly looking for new fields of employment. While giants such as IBM or HP disconnect from hardware development wherever possible, the AWS with Echo is currently presenting something tangible. There will probably be further developments in this direction.

Amazon has also just entered the market for television series and films. This will probably not be the last surprising step for Jeff Bezos' company.

WHY AMAZON WEB SERVICES (AWS)?

Amazon Web Services (AWS) is a collection of various web services from the online retailer Amazon.com that started in 2006. Numerous popular applications such as Dropbox, Foursquare, or Netflix use the services of Amazon Web Services. In addition to Microsoft Windows Azure and Google Cloud Platform, AWS is one of the most important international offerings in cloud computing and is described as a pioneer in the industry . 1

In my view, cloud computing in this dimension has the following advantages.

Benefits

- 100% variable costs

With cloud computing, you only pay for the resources that you actually use. You have no initial investment costs and, therefore, no tied-up capital.

- Automation

AWS is 100% automatable. The management of the entire IT can be programmed. This reduces human errors. You will also receive the exact documentation of your entire IT (firewall, user rights, ...).

- Increase speed and agility

A new server is available in AWS within a few minutes. Start experiments with minimal effort. Amazon and AWS are very innovative. Benefit from innovative technologies.

- Flexible capacity

You never have to estimate the capacity for the next few years. If you need more resources, they are available within a few minutes. If you need fewer resources, you can switch them off immediately. You only pay for the resources you actually need. For example, you can increase resources during the day and decrease them at night.

- Benefiting from

economies of scale are a basic concept in business administration. AWS provides hundreds of thousands of customers with computing resources and achieves economies of scale that you cannot achieve on your own.

- Focus on customers

You focus on your customers while AWS takes care of their servers. Do not deal with the operation of data centers and servers but with the wishes of your customers.

- Worldwide

AWS has had its own region in Germany (Frankfurt) since October 23. Together with the region in Ireland, you have the possibility to operate your IT at two locations within Europe for maximum security. Together with the regions in Brazil, Japan, Singapore, China, and the USA, AWS now has a total of 11 regions to supply your global business with IT.

- Professional partner

AWS fulfills the regulations and standards: HIPAA, SOC 1 & 2 & 3, PCI DSS Level 1, DIN ISO / IEC 27001, IT Grundschutz, FedRAMP (SM), DIACAP and FISMA, ITAR, FIPS 140-2, CSA , MPAA 2 . The use of AWS can be designed in accordance with BDSG.

AWS ELASTIC BEANSTALK

AWS Elastic Beanstalk is a cloud deployment service that automates the deployment of applications on the Amazon Web Services (AWS) infrastructure.

To use the service, developers only need to upload their applications. Provisioning, load balancing, auto-scaling, and monitoring of the application status are carried out automatically.

Elastic Beanstalk supports web applications developed in Java, Node.js, PHP, Python, Ruby, and .NET, among others, as well as web development stacks. The open architecture of Elastic Beanstalk also allows non-Internet applications to be deployed to Elastic Beanstalk.

The AWS Toolkit for Visual Studio and the AWS Toolkit for Eclipse enable developers to deploy and manage applications from within the integrated development environment (IDE). Programmers can select infrastructure management elements for management when needed.

An application created locally by a developer can be made available on the Internet in a few minutes after programming with Elastic Beanstalk. All the developer has to do is upload the code. Elastic Beanstalk then automatically takes over the deployment. This means that development teams can concentrate on building their applications and do not have to worry about managing the infrastructure.

In addition to being easy to deploy, Elastic Beanstalk offers a number of other useful features: the cloud service enables full access to the underlying resources, support for monitoring and notifications, access to log files without having to log in to the instances, and the ability to configure application servers, versioning, or rollback.

AWS users can also use AWS Elastic Beanstalk to develop PHP applications on Amazon Elastic Compute Cloud (EC2) instances and perform further version deployments on the existing stack.

There is no separate fee for AWS Elastic Beanstalk - customers pay for the resources needed to store and run their applications.

CLOUD COMPUTING - WHAT IS BEHIND IT?

Setting up your own data center is time-consuming and costly: skilled personnel is required for the acquisition and maintenance. In addition, you can never scale as needed. After all, your company should grow, and therefore your IT must always be one step ahead. For this reason, you often provide more resources than the employees currently need. After all, a functioning data center is vital for most companies. If it fails, the work stops. And nobody can afford that, so you have to spend too much rather than too little at the data center.

With cloud computing, you go a different way: Instead of purchasing, installing, and maintaining the technology yourself, you can use web services. A wide variety of services are available in a data center via the Internet: it is possible to obtain storage space, computing power (i.e., processor power), databases or software environments via the Internet. In most cases, this form of modern outsourcing runs through a rental model. Capacities can be easily booked in this way - and promptly when you really need them.

History of cloud computing

Networking computers to give more users more computing power and storage space is not a new invention. Back in the 1950s, mainframes had taken a step towards cloud computing. At that time, users could access the mainframe and use their capacities via several terminals within the organization (in companies or universities). In the beginning, however, as timeshare: users had to reserve computing time and were allowed to use the power of the mainframe for their calculations.

In the following decades, virtualization was then developed: Now, computing instances could be reproduced in an abstract, purely virtual manner. With the invention of the Internet, such virtualized environments were finally available to everyone online. Since the 1990s, such models have also been commercially available for a larger mass of users.

At that time, the term cloud became more popular. But it was only in the new millennium that companies and private individuals began to become increasingly interested in technology. The first cloud offerings were still individual services: storage space for exchanging files, for example, or Google's spreadsheet or documents, in which several users can work together on a document. At the same time, Amazon began to make its huge server farms available to other users: Amazon Web Services (AWS) enable other companies to use the infrastructure of the e-commerce giant and run software there.

Cloud computing is now part of everyday life for numerous people. Most smartphones - or more broadly: the Internet of Things - are in constant contact with the cloud. Users take a photo with the smartphone's camera and automatically upload the image to the Apple or Google cloud so that they can be accessed with another device.

What is cloud computing?

In principle, cloud computing is only a collective term: This describes the offer of hardware and software over the Internet. It does not specify the extent to which the services must be provided - from simple cloud storage, in which users receive storage capacity on remote servers in addition to their own hard disk space, to the infrastructure in the cloud, through which companies have complete data centers via the Internet Respectively.

Definition of cloud computing

The collective term cloud computing describes the provision of various hardware and software solutions over the Internet. Processor performance, storage space, and software environments can be rented by users as needed to expand or replace their own infrastructure.

According to a paper by the National Institute of Standards and Technology (NIST), offerings called cloud computing must meet certain characteristics:

On-demand self-service: It should be possible for users to be able to independently request the required resources without having to contact an employee of the provider each time.

Broad Network Access: Access to cloud computing works over the Internet. No unusual techniques or protocols may be used. The use of standardized methods ensures that all users have easy access to the service.

Resource pooling: The merging of several computing instances is the basic prerequisite for cloud computing. Such pools are usually used in the form of server farms to supply several users with computing power or storage capacity at the same time. It is rarely clear to the customer which device he is actually using: The capacities are allocated dynamically.

Rapid elasticity: The delivery of capacities has to be quick and needs-based. At best, automatisms are active that switch resources on or off without the help of customers or employees.

Measured Service: The use of the cloud offer is monitored at all times. This creates more transparency for both the provider and the user.

Cloud computing is often understood as an attempt to make computing available in the same way as is known from other infrastructural services: water comes from the tap, electricity from the socket, and computing power from the Internet. Just like most people do not need to know how an electricity company works, you no longer need to understand how a computer is composed through cloud computing. The user consumes the resources (storage space, computing power) just like the electricity and receives a corresponding invoice for this.

As the E-Werk in the center of the power grid, cloud computing usually starts from a large data center or server farm. Many computers (or servers) are connected here, and resources are pooled. This grid computing achieves high performance. In combination with virtualizations, individual virtual instances can be created for individual users within the network. The individual user does not know which device his files are on and does not have to: Access works quickly and easily without this knowledge.

Variants of cloud computing

The market now includes a wide variety of offers. These differ - apart from the price and the support services - above all in terms of their shift and deployment models. The term "shifts" refers to the scope of the service, and the delivery model characterizes the type of offer.

Layer model

One layer corresponds to a certain service level: The various "as-a-Service" levels or layers describe the scope of the offer. Therefore, they are usually represented in a pyramid model. While Infrastructure as a Service is the largest, Software as a Service only focuses on certain applications.

Infrastructure as a Service (IaaS):At this level, the provider offers complete hardware solutions: processor performance, storage space, and network technology. The instances that the user uses are completely virtual and are divided into the resource pool. IaaS can serve as the basis for the other layers but is also offered as a single product.

Platform as a Service (PaaS): This layer goes one step further by not only providing the hardware but a complete environment. PaaS is primarily aimed at software developers. The provider ensures an already set up development environment in the cloud, on hosted hardware. Programmers save the need to set up and maintain the environment.

Software as a Service (SaaS): In the highest layer, users are offered complete software from the cloud. SaaS is, therefore, primarily aimed at normal end-users. They no longer have to worry about the installation and maintenance of the software and can also be sure that the performance of the hardware is sufficient for the smooth execution of the software. To access the software, users either use a web browser or a restricted program that loads most of it from the cloud.

Everything as a Service (XaaS): In addition to the three layers mentioned, other services are advertised again and again by providers. In principle, this only happens for marketing reasons. A XaaS can actually always be assigned to a different layer or has nothing at all to do with cloud computing: Humans as a Service (HuaaS), for example, describes a form of crowdsourcing. A pool of people takes over work over the Internet.

Deployment Models

The deployment models describe the type of offer: Are instances reserved for only one user or company, or do you share the pool with other people? The deployment model results from the answer to this question.

Private cloud: The servers are used exclusively by one customer. A private cloud can but does not have to be on-site (internal cloud). Even with a hosting provider with a server farm, it is possible to use dedicated hardware to which other customers of the provider have no access.

Community Cloud: The Community Cloud works in a similar way to a private cloud, but with this model, several customers share a dedicated hardware instance. The composition of the users is not chosen at random, but several customers - mostly from the same business area or with similar interests - come together in a targeted manner. The Community Cloud can also be managed either in a company or externally. The goal is to achieve savings compared to multiple private clouds.

Public cloud: This type of provision corresponds to the actual idea behind a cloud. A server network is used together with the general public. Who uses which hardware is not visible to the user and cannot be determined by him.

Hybrid cloud: This is a hybrid of the two models of private and public cloud. A company or a private user decides to leave a certain part of the operation (e.g., security-related aspects) in the private environment and to choose the public cloud for other parts.

This is cloud computing

Hardware and software no longer have to be bought and operated by yourself. You can also rent IT. Most of the providers of these IT services are geographically distant, so the data and applications are no longer on your company's local computer but in the cloud. This does not mean that your data is wandering around unsecured so that everyone can access it. It just means that your data is no longer stored directly with you, but away from the company center. Of course, you always have access to your data. And only you. The advantages here are more flexibility, scalability, and low costs since there is no separate server structure.

Do you think that is not the case with you? Not correct! As soon as you have an e-mail address on the Internet, enter your username and password there, you are a user of a cloud provider. Other examples would be:

- dropbox
- Microsoft OneDrive
- Google Drive
- Amazon Drive
- iCloud

However, when choosing your "cloud provider," you should make sure that all relevant security regulations are met. By the way, the world's strictest security requirements apply in Germany, which is why many companies choose a cloud " Made in Germany."

WHAT TYPES OF CLOUD COMPUTING ARE THERE?

There are three different types of cloud computing: Infrastructure as a service, Platform as a service, Software as a service. These are differentiated according to the depth of the outsourcing.

Infrastructure as a service (IaaS)

IaaS forms the base layer for all other cloud service models. Here, virtual infrastructure components (e.g., computing power, network capacity, and backup systems) can be used as required. The computing and storage performance takes place on virtualized servers, and the scope can be adapted at any time by the company using it. IaaS is a solution for companies that have to cover peak loads (suddenly high demand for electricity) more frequently. To do this, it would be too expensive to invest in additional IT infrastructure, and costs for IT administration are also saved. The current largest and most important players in the IaaS market include

- Amazon Web Services (AWS)
- Google Compute Engine
- Microsoft Azure
- IBM Cloud Services

The "Big Four" now cover more than 50 percent of the market for virtual IT resources, and the trend is rising.

Platform as a service (PaaS)

PaaS users are a cloud model for system architects and application developers and have access to a development environment or framework in which they can develop and operate their own applications. However, the development process itself and the programming take place outside the company. Components, in addition to IaaS are the necessary runtime environment, which includes the middleware between the operating system and the actual applications as well as the operating system. Only the applications and data storage are still operated on the company's servers. Here, too, the computing and data capacities can be individually adapted to the needs of the company. The providers of PaaS include

- Google App Engine

- Amazon Elastic Beanstalk
- Microsoft Azure
- Force.com

Software as a service (SaaS)

SaaS is the most comprehensive cloud service model, ranging from outsourcing a single application to outsourcing the entire corporate IT. Here, the applications and data are even in the cloud and thus on the servers of the cloud provider. The user rents the software from the Internet as "software on demand" and only pays for the modules that are actually used. This makes it very inexpensive for the user, from which it follows that this is the most used software module. The range of SaaS solutions from the cloud ranges from office and collaboration solutions to business software for CRM and ERP, such as weclapp.

Advantages of SaaS:

✓ Cost savings for IT resources because the data is

stored and backed up in the cloud ✓ The company using it does not have to worry about updates

✓ Completely location-independent ✓ No cumbersome migration due to release changes or updates - scale the booked software according to specific needs and Payment only for the level of use.

TRADITIONAL SOFTWARE LICENSING VS. SAAS - WHAT ARE THE DIFFERENCES?

CLASSIC IT (ON SERVICES)SAAS (ON DEMAND)

The installation The software is installed and implemented at the customer's site. A scalable IT infrastructure is available to the customer without installation.

The data center (RZ) Servers and storage are located in the data center, or server room of the customer and both the system and application software, and all data are stored here.The hardware is located in the data center of the provider and can no longer be specifically assigned to the customer. The high-performance hardware and state-of-the-art backup procedures make failure almost impossible.

The modules Customer purchases modules and has to pay license fees for them. All applications are stored as dynamic resources on the servers and organized in a highly available manner.

The payment   Fees are completely separate from the actual usage of the application. (Royalties)   The customer only pays for the functions and services that they actually need.

CREATION OF THE CLOUD

Cloud storage here and data from the cloud there - everyone is talking about "the cloud." But what is cloud storage?

In fact, the concept of the cloud is not as new as most think: There were first ideas in this regard in the 1950s. At that time, however, the technical requirements for cloud computing were still missing. At the end of the 1990s, technology was finally ready, software-as-a-service (SaaS) was now possible. At SaaS, an IT service provider operates software that the user can use via a web browser without installing it on their own computer. The user, therefore, does not have to worry about licenses or updates to the software.

The cloud technology today

In parallel to the ever faster bandwidths and better technical equipment, the cloud concept also developed further. More and more IT service providers are offering storage space on their servers and online services for a fee. The saved files are always accessible online, which means you can access them from anywhere. This is useful if you want to access photos, documents, and other data both at home, in the office or on the go.

Where does the term "cloud" come from?

What does cloud actually mean? The term cloud comes from English; it simply translates into German "cloud." The cloud was used by information technicians in structural drawings of networks to identify systems that were part of their own network but were operated externally. The structure and function of these external systems were irrelevant to your own network. Today, you store files in a location, the exact function and structure of which is also not relevant, the cloud. Nevertheless, you know from the term how the product works: data is distributed to different servers and can be called up online from anywhere - you only need Internet access.

How does cloud technology work?

Now, after the question "What is a cloud?" is answered, the next question immediately arises: How exactly does it work? The basic principle can be explained as follows:

A service provider makes his servers available to customers in the form of a virtual data center. To do this, many servers are interconnected so that the data is no longer stored on just one server. The storage resources can be called up as required; The user has online access to the cloud at any time, in which he can store any amount of data.

What forms of cloud computing are there?

Cloud technology comes in various forms. You are already using the SaaS cloud computing mentioned above in the form of a browser-based e-mail service such as FreeMail. The virtual data center offers storage capacities and application programs that you can use to their full extent via a browser - even without installation. Another form is cloud computing via Platform-as-a-Service (PaaS), which provides programming environments with adaptable computing and data capacities. Users develop their own software on this platform. Finally, there is Infrastructure-as-a-Service (IaaS), where users access hardware resources such as computers, networks, and storage - you are effectively renting your own server.

What makes the cloud so popular?

Anyone who has ever been annoyed about irrevocably deleted data will appreciate the convenience of a cloud. If you use cloud storage to back up your data, you no longer have to fear broken hard drives, lost USB sticks, and faulty files. Your data is always safe in the cloud. You can access them anytime, anywhere via the Internet; Your data remains private: you determine who has access to your cloud. If you want to share certain data with others, you can do it with just a few clicks. Share your vacation photos in seconds with family members and friends or set up a folder that is accessible to all for your colleagues. Many cloud offers are offered free of charge with little storage. This storage can then usually be expanded flexibly at an affordable price.

This is how cloud hosting works

Private, public, or hybrid cloud?

Cloud hosting is offered in three variants - as a service in a private, public, or hybrid cloud.

Hosting in a private cloud is similar to that of a classic dedicated server. Only a single customer uses the infrastructure and therefore operates his own cloud. This variant is usually used by larger companies that expect a high level of security from such a solution.

With a public cloud, hosters make their server resources available to a larger number of customers. Depending on the peak loads, free resources are used by various customers or additionally activated. This model enables extremely high scalability for customers. Every cloud user receives the optimal hosting performance for them. In the case of many contract variants for public cloud hosting, only the service that was called up is billed at exactly the exact hour.

Some companies want the flexibility of a cloud, but the only trust dedicated servers to trust key applications. These then often opt for a hybrid cloud solution. For permanent loads, they rely on the undivided resources of dedicated systems because they hope that this will ensure constant performance. They use cloud resources as a flexible load overflow.

The basic idea of the public cloud: flexible and scalable

This shows that the basic idea of cloud computing is actually only realized in the public cloud. A cloud provider has resources that all customers share! Every member of the cloud community gets its optimal hosting performance. Ideally, customers of cloud hosting can also freely configure and scale all applications as well as hardware and software options. Processor performance, memory, or hard disk size - in a public cloud, it is possible to adapt all relevant server parameters to ongoing operations. Some providers have already automated these adjustment processes in such a way that the administration effort has been considerably reduced: This is called "auto-scaling". If hosting customers really only pay for the resources actually used according to the "pay-as-you-use" principle instead of for a complete server, cloud hosting is often an inexpensive alternative to conventional hosting. It is particularly user-friendly if resources that are not used can be "frozen." Then the usage price will drop significantly in some cases.

Three central elements of cloud computing

Cloud hosting is based on the three central elements of cloud computing: Infrastructure-as-a-Service (IaaS), Platform-as-a-Service (PaaS), and Software-as-a-Service (SaaS). The hardware resources required for a hosting project are made available as Infrastructure-as-a-

Service (IaaS) over the Internet. This level is often referred to as "instances." PaaS is based on the instances: These are usually working environments for the development of online applications such as web servers, middleware, or databases. The services from SaaS are supplemented, i.e., by applications that are usually immediately ready for use and can be rented.

Cloud hosting not only opens up new opportunities for website-based projects. The individually available, highly scalable services also drive innovations in other business applications. Via IaaS, PaaS, and SaaS, for example, virtual workstations or automated archives with sophisticated backup systems can be set up. Solutions in the cloud are also on the rise with enterprise resource planning (ERP). Because with these IT solutions, the value creation process can always be planned and controlled according to requirements.

Security in the cloud

One question still concerns IT experts: Is cloud hosting really secure?

The threats to web projects in the cloud are typically no greater than the risks to projects on other hosting infrastructures.

THE ADVANTAGES OF CLOUD COMPUTING FOR PRIVATE USERS

The advantages are that they do not need their own hardware resources for data storage or use of the application software, as they are made available via the cloud. Users can also use the respective cloud service with different devices, whether mobile or stationary.

THE DISADVANTAGES

These are particularly in the area of security. One of the reasons is the continuously recurring attacks by hackers on the servers of renowned cloud providers such as Amazon or Google in order to capture personal users and other data. In addition, in most cases, to use cloud services, a lot of sensitive data must be stored, which of course, is stored and passed on for the use of the service. If this work with the data for most cloud providers also takes place within the framework of applicable data protection guidelines, the EU citizen is "smeared," however, who makes use of services that have neither their headquarters nor their servers placed in the EU area.

THE BENEFITS OF CLOUD STORAGE FOR BUSINESSES

The focus here is, in particular, on the cost savings that companies can generate by saving in some cases, substantial investments by renting services in the cloud from external service providers. Such a procedure enables savings in terms of personnel as well as in terms of the hardware used. In addition, no long-term capital commitment is required since all costs are usually billed monthly and can, therefore, be calculated well.

THE DISADVANTAGES

In this context, the dependency on the provider should be mentioned; for example, if he or she does not take good care of his customers or cannot provide sufficient capacity. The question of how to handle sensitive, company-related data also needs an answer. The quality of the Internet connection must also be taken into account, as the high-speed Internet can often not yet be used, particularly in rural areas. After all, a perfectly functioning internet is an essential prerequisite for using cloud computing.

SOME FREE CLOUD PROVIDERS

To put it straight away: What all cloud storage, whether free or paid, has in common, as already mentioned, is the security vulnerability with regard to the data, since it resides on third-party servers and "migrates" through the Internet when it is uploaded and downloaded. Therefore, highly sensitive data should not be stored on the World Wide Web at all.

Free providers of cloud storage from Germany are examples

- Web.de
- E-Post Cloud,
- Telekom Cloud
- tuxedo
- Strato HiDrive Free

PAID PROVIDERS

Benefits:

- Extremely user-friendly
- Secure end-to-end encryption
- Fast support

Disadvantage:

- This service is too expensive for private users.
- Another is " lucky cloud, "which costs 1.99 euros per month.

Benefits:

- Any sync folder
- Secure end-to-end encryption
- File Version History

Disadvantage:

- Encryption is only possible via the client.
- The user has to pay 9.50 euros per month for the LeitzCloud .

Advantage:

- User-friendly desktop client
- Comprehensive services
- Flexible pricing system

Disadvantage:

- The disadvantage of this provider is the lack of a web office.

CLASSIFICATIONS OF
ROLES IN THE CLOUD

There are four types of user roles in cloud computing. On the one hand, there are SaaS users, i.e., those companies, employees, and also private users who use a SaaS service. There is also talk of the SaaS providers who provide their services to SaaS users. The SaaS providers are also assigned the role of the cloud user, since they use the services of the third user role, namely the cloud providers. A cloud provider actually stands for the cloud operator, who usually owns the data center and the entire infrastructure that goes with it. The SaaS provider can use the data center to make its services available to the SaaS user via the infrastructure.

Classifications of roles in the cloud [1]

In some cases, the cloud provider can take on the role of the SaaS provider at the same time. This is exactly the case if the operator of the data center also offers SaaS services directly. In the same way, however, a SaaS user can also take on the role of a cloud user, namely precisely when he is outsourcing all of his server capacities (storage, computing capacity, etc.) directly to the data center of a cloud provider.

In general, it can be said that the problems of the respective roles are shifting. The SaaS user shifts his 'problems' in the form of software and services to the SaaS provider, which in turn outsources his 'problems' to the cloud provider in the form of a data center.

Platform as a service

Platform as a Service (PaaS) is the middle tier of the cloud computing service model and goes one step further than IaaS. It is responsible for providing a transparent development environment. The third-party provider provides a platform on which (web) applications can be developed, tested, and hosted. The applications are then executed on the provider's infrastructure and use their resources. The complete life cycle of an application can be fully managed through it. The services on the platform of the respective provider can be addressed via APIs. The advantage is that small companies, in particular, can keep their development infrastructure to a minimum. You only need a desktop PC, a web browser, possibly a local IDE, an internet connection, and their knowledge to develop applications. The rest is the responsibility of the third-party provider who is responsible for the infrastructure (operating system, web server, development environment, etc.). Here too, billing is based on the principle of pay use.

ADVANTAGES AND DISADVANTAGES OF CLOUD COMPUTING

Before introducing cloud computing programs, you should consider the following advantages and disadvantages and compare whether this could even fit your own needs and requirements:

10 advantages of cloud computing

① cost saving

The use of cloud computing eliminates costly investments in your own IT infrastructures. The company also saves expensive investments in business software because it only pays for the functions that it actually uses.

② Scalability

Companies can quickly adapt functions to changing needs in terms of quantity and quality . Complex upgrade procedures for the implementation of new applications are a thing of the past.

③ High availability

Technology at the highest level in the data centers of the cloud providers guarantees the highest possible availability of applications and data . In order to achieve a comparable availability level of 99.9 percent, a company would otherwise have to invest considerable sums.

④ Improve collaboration

Cooperation on projects is significantly simplified. Through location-independent shared access , project processes can be accelerated, the workflow significantly improved, and everyone involved is always up-to-date through real-time updates of documents .

⑤ Automatic updates

There are no longer update procedures for company applications or release changes with cumbersome data migrations. Functions are continuously updated automatically so that all modules used in a cloud application are always up to date .

⑥ Relief for IT administration

Data backups are no longer necessary for cloud computing because they are carried out automatically by the cloud provider. The reduced operating and maintenance effort for IT resources relieves IT administration in the company and helps to save costs.

⑦ Concentration on the core business

By relieving the IT department of troublesome routine tasks , the company can concentrate even better on its core business, improve competitiveness and increase its growth opportunities.

⑧ Location independence

Users can access their applications and data anywhere in the world where an internet connection is available. This increases their flexibility and gives them a decisive competitive advantage .

⑨ Competitive advantages for SMEs

Thanks to cloud computing, even small companies can use the powerful functions of CRM and ERP systems that would not be affordable with an on-premises solution. The possibility of use enables SMEs to improve their competitive situation sustainably .

⑩ environmental friendliness

The use of cloud computing conserves resources because servers and other IT resources in the data centers are flexibly scaled and thus used to maximum capacity. This reduces the power consumption and improves the CO_2 balance .

1. CLOUD COMPUTING IS SCALABLE AND HIGH-PERFORMANCE IT

The most obvious advantage of cloud computing is the scalability of virtual IT resources: They are available at any time at any size - with a click of the mouse or automatically. Whether storage space, processor performance, RAM or software licenses, you can add anything to any extent and switch it off again.

With cloud computing, you don't have to keep idle IT resources at peak times. At the same time, you can also easily handle strong and unexpected or unplanned usage loads and fulfill service level agreements at any time. Thanks to the optimal technical equipment and broadband network connection of your cloud provider's data center, you also benefit from increased performance and IT availability.

2. CLOUD COMPUTING SAVES COSTS & REDUCES INVESTMENTS

The second - also very noticeable - advantage of cloud computing is the cost saving: Because only as many IT resources are used as required, there are no fixed costs for "idle" hardware or software licenses. In addition, IT resources in the cloud are cheaper for you as an entrepreneur because the basic costs (acquisition, operation, maintenance) are shared by several users.

Capital that is no longer tied up by high fixed costs can in turn be invested in the company in the development of products, optimization of value chains or business model innovation.

3. CLOUD COMPUTING ENABLES INNOVATIONS

The use of cloud computing creates completely new spaces for experimentation: You can try out new value chains or develop and test completely new business models without major investments in IT infrastructures or the risk of long-term contracts. For small and medium-sized enterprises (SMEs) in particular, this means unprecedented freedom and reduces access barriers to other markets and target groups. In addition, you can integrate and implement new solutions more quickly within the company.

4. CLOUD COMPUTING FACILITATES COOPERATION

The organizational flexibility of cloud computing is another advantage: cloud-based cooperation enables new cross-company value chains. This enables you to increase your efficiency internally in the company and, together with partners, offer products or services that you could not implement on your own.

5. CLOUD COMPUTING TECHNOLOGY GROWS WITH THE MARKET

The innovation cycles of software are getting shorter and shorter. Very few companies are able to keep pace with their own development resources or even be a leader at this speed. The need-based rental of appropriate virtual infrastructure shifts this pressure to innovate to the IT service provider. As a company, you can concentrate on the central aspects of your value chains and move secondary ones - such as Infrastructure as a Service (IaaS) - to the cloud. The cloud computing provider is responsible for new hardware, updates to existing software and quantitative and qualitative further development of resources.

6. CLOUD COMPUTING REMAINS COMPATIBLE

Cloud computing is on the way to becoming standard technology. All large companies and groups rely on virtualized IT solutions. Cloud-based product strategies will already achieve the greatest compatibility on the market in the medium term, standards beyond cloud computing, on the other hand, will quickly become obsolete (depending on the industry) and will no longer be served by relevant business partners.

7. CLOUD COMPUTING INCREASES DATA SECURITY & DATA PROTECTION

The greatest concerns about cloud computing are expressed in terms of data protection and data security . In fact, you can significantly increase your information security in the company through cloud computing. Because commissioned IT service providers are much better able to keep technology and organization constantly up to date and to meet legal requirements at all times. In addition, as a company you save corresponding costs for investments, updates, further training, certifications etc.

Better products and services: Positive customer experiences largely depend on how fast, comprehensive and location-independent information of all kinds is available and usable. Efficient supply chains, customer services, sales etc. thrive on this. Cloud services can be unbeatable in doing just that and thus generating decisive market advantages. Innovative solutions such as AI-based chatbots can also be better developed and used in the cloud. So-called microservices also make it possible to adapt or replace IT components with little effort during operation. The cloud also facilitates implementation in the Internet of Things (IoT).

Flexibility: IT actually serves companies to be faster, more agile, more error-free, in short: better prepared for the challenges of the market. But developments are not only accelerating on the market side - the cycles of digital products are also becoming shorter and shorter technologically. What was still state of the art yesterday will often not even be upgradable tomorrow. While operational IT with on-premise solutions has to lag behind these processes, it can concentrate on the actual business in cloud computing because both the updating and scaling of the cloud services are the responsibility of the provider.

Cost reduction: A number of investments in IT infrastructure that would otherwise tie up capital are eliminated. Depending on the contract, the effort for the services can be agreed depending on usage (p ay as you go) . In general, these monthly or yearly costs are considerably lower than with on-premise solutions, which have to be dimensioned according to peak loads.

Data security: Even if cloud computing can never guarantee 100 percent security, the security features of large providers rank among the best that can be obtained on the market. Small and medium-sized companies in particular like to underestimate the risk of becoming a direct victim of a cyber attack (not to mention their own human error), but are generally technically much worse compared to cloud providers against data loss, failures, corrupted systems, etc. . protected and able to get a complete data recovery at short notice.

Data protection compliance: In principle, companies remain responsible for the proper processing of (personal) data within the meaning of the General Data Protection Regulation (GDPR) even if they use a cloud service provider. Data protection-compliant IT is also guaranteed (and possibly also at a higher level) if the necessary conditions are met. Above all, this includes that the cloud service itself fulfills all the requirements of GDPR compliance, that this has been contractually agreed to be watertight and that the company ensures that there are no irregularities in data traffic.

Saving resources and using them more efficiently: With cloud computing, the effort for hardware (data center, server room ...) is partially eliminated, for software largely. This saves companies internally from purchasing, installing, configuring, maintaining and updating software. Cloud-based services are also much easier to use regardless of location, for example via mobile devices. This enables z. B. Sales and service representatives to realize better customer experiences. Teams can work on tasks or projects seamlessly and without delay, even beyond an existing intranet. The core business is relieved of the coordination effort with the operational IT.

Consistent data: Especially with complex processes in the company, the consistency of data is vital. The enormous susceptibility to errors in decentralized storage, processing and transfer of data without these processes being perfectly synchronized can cause massive operational problems. This risk is reduced to a minimum in cloud computing and is therefore another important advantage; Files are always identical here, even if they are accessed from different interfaces. Even managing simultaneous access to the same file is technically possible.

Simplification: The usability of many cloud-based applications is less complex because processes are moved to the background that are not immediately necessary for the purpose of the application. A prominent example: the development of products, apps and other software on cloud-based platforms (PaaS).

Big data management: In scientific research, for market analyzes, in the health sector and in a number of other areas of application, it is increasingly important to collect, network and analyze extremely large amounts of data and then to visualize them in a way that is conducive to action or to make them otherwise detectable. The computing effort for this is hardly or not at all possible without the performance, flexibility and versatility of the cloud, but at least not so efficiently.

In general , a good 96 percent said in the study mentioned that they were mostly or very satisfied with the results of their cloud migration . 55 percent found a positive effect "immediately" or "after a short time". Many existing data centers from before the cloud are still running, but half of the companies surveyed already intend to source infrastructure services exclusively from the cloud in the future, while only around 20 percent want the existing data center to continue operating.

Disadvantages of cloud computing

✗ Internet connection as a basic requirement

Since all transfers and accesses go through the internet , a stable and fast internet connection is a basic requirement for effective cloud computing. However, the bandwidths required for smooth work in the cloud are not yet available across the board. This can lead to unsightly delays. When choosing a cloud provider , you should therefore not only pay attention to its size, but also to its infrastructure .

Verlust loss of control

All data will be stored outside of the company. In order to avoid data protection risks with cloud providers in the USA and some other countries, you should make sure when choosing the cloud provider that it operates its data centers in Germany. Even then, many companies still see the lack of control as a major disadvantage in cloud computing. This can also be regulated through corresponding compliance agreements in the usage contracts with the cloud provider.

Downtime

Downtime is often described as one of the biggest disadvantages of cloud computing. Since cloud computing systems are Internet-based, service outages are always an unfortunate option and can occur for any reason.

Can your company afford the impact of a failure or slowdown? A failure of Amazon Web Services in 2017 cost listed companies up to $ 150 million and no company is immune, especially if it can't afford to disrupt critical business processes.

The best ways to minimize planned downtime in a cloud environment:

Develop services with high availability and disaster recovery in mind. Use the multi-availability zones of the cloud providers in your infrastructure.

If your services are not resilient, consider multi-regional implementations with automated failover to ensure the best possible business continuity.

Define and implement a disaster recovery plan in accordance with your business goals that provide the lowest possible recovery time (RTO) and recovery point goals (RPO).

Consider implementing dedicated connectivity like AWS Direct Connect, Azure ExpressRoute, or Google Cloud's Dedicated Interconnect or Partner Interconnect. These services establish a dedicated network connection between you and the cloud service point-of-point. This can reduce the risk of business interruption through the public Internet.

Security and data protection

Any discussion of data needs to deal with security and privacy, especially when it comes to managing sensitive data. We mustn't forget what happened to Code Space and hacking their AWS EC2 console, which resulted in data deletion and ultimately closure. Their dependence on a remote cloud-based infrastructure meant that they had to take the risks of outsourcing.

Of course, every cloud service provider is expected to manage and secure the underlying hardware infrastructure of a deployment. However, your responsibilities are in the area of user access management, and it is up to you to carefully consider all risk scenarios.

Although the recent public credit card and user credential violations are still fresh in the memory, steps have been taken to ensure the security of the data. An example of this is the General Data Protection Regulation (GDPR), which was recently adopted in the European Union to give users more control over their data. However, you must be aware of your responsibilities and follow good practices.

The best measures to minimize security and data protection risks:

- Understand the shared responsibility model of your cloud provider.
- Implement security at all levels of your deployment.
- Know who should have access to every resource and service and limit access to the least privileges.
- Make sure your team's skills are up to the task: Sound security knowledge for your cloud teams is one of the best ways to mitigate security and privacy concerns in the cloud.

- Take a risk-based approach to securing assets that are used in the cloud.
- Extend security to the device.
- Implementation of multi-factor authentication for all accounts that access sensitive data or systems.

Vulnerability to attack

In cloud computing, every component is online, which reveals potential weak points . Even the best teams experience severe attacks and security breaches from time to time. Because cloud computing is designed as a public service, it's easy to use before you learn to walk. After all, no one at a cloud provider checks your administrative skills before granting you an account: all you have to do is usually a valid credit card.

The best measures to help you reduce cloud attacks:

- Make security a key aspect of all IT operations.
- Keep ALL your teams up to date with best practices for cloud security.
- Ensure that security policies and procedures are regularly checked and reviewed.
- Proactive classification of information and application of access controls.

- Use cloud services such as AWS Inspector, AWS CloudWatch, AWS CloudTrail and AWS Config to automate compliance controls.
- Prevent data exfiltration.
- Integration of prevention and response strategies in security operations.
- Discover rogue projects with audits.
- Remove password access from accounts that don't need to sign in to services.
- Check and turn the access key and access data.
- Follow the security blogs and announcements to stay informed of known attacks.
- Apply proven security measures to any open source software you use.

These practices help your organization monitor the exposure and movement of critical data, protect critical systems from attacks and compromises, and authenticate access to infrastructure and data to protect yourself from further risks.

Limited control and flexibility

To varying degrees (depending on the service), cloud users may find that they have less control over the function and execution of services within the cloud-hosted infrastructure. The end-user license agreement and the management guidelines of a cloud provider can limit the possibilities of the customers for their implementations. Customers retain control over their applications, data, and services, but may not have the same control over their back-end infrastructure.

The best measures to maintain control and flexibility:

- Consider hiring a cloud provider partner to help you implement, run, and support cloud services.

- Understanding your responsibilities and the responsibilities of the cloud provider in the shared responsibility model reduces the likelihood of omissions or errors.

- Take the time to understand the basic support level of your cloud service provider. Does this service level meet your support requirements? Most cloud providers offer additional support levels in addition to basic support at an additional cost.

- Make sure you understand the Service Level Agreement (SLA), which relates to the infrastructure and services that you will use, and how this affects your agreements with your customers.

Supplier relationships

Supplier loyalty is another perceived disadvantage of cloud computing. Differences between provider platforms can lead to difficulties when migrating from one cloud platform to another, which can be associated with additional costs and configuration complexity. Gaps or compromises made during migration can also result in your data being exposed to additional security and data protection vulnerabilities.

The best measures to reduce dependency:

- Design considering the best measures for cloud architectures. All cloud services offer the opportunity to improve availability and performance, to decouple layers and to reduce performance bottlenecks. If you've built your services with best practices for cloud architectures, you're less likely to experience porting issues from one cloud platform to another.
- If you understand exactly what your suppliers are selling, you can avoid lock-in challenges.
- The use of a multi-cloud strategy is another way to avoid binding providers. While this can increase the development and operational

complexity of your implementations, it doesn't have to be a deal breaker. Training can help teams prepare for the development and selection of appropriate services and technologies.

- Strategically build flexibility in application development to ensure portability now and in the future.

Costs

The use of cloud solutions on a small scale and for short-term projects can be perceived as expensive. Pay-as-you-go cloud services can offer more flexibility and lower hardware costs, but the total price could be higher than expected. Until you are sure what works best for you, it is a good idea to experiment with a variety of offers. You can also use cost calculators from providers such as Amazon Web Services and Google Cloud Platform.

The best cost reduction measures:

- Try not to deploy too much instead of using auto-scaling services.
- Scaling both down and up.

- Prepayment if you have a known minimum usage.
- Stop your instances when they are not in use.
- Create alerts to track spending in the cloud.
- It is best to try not to deploy too much instead of using auto-scaling services.

Disadvantages of cloud computing: final thoughts

Many companies benefit from the agility, scalability and pay-per-use billing that cloud services offer. As with any infrastructure service, however, the suitability of cloud computing for your specific use case should be assessed in a risk-based assessment. Build in time for research and planning to understand how the cloud will affect your business.

ADVANTAGES AND DISADVANTAGES OF CLOUD HOSTING FOR COMPANIES

Whether infrastructure, supplement to everyday business or a clever software solution: Many companies rely on cloud hosting to relieve their own IT department. If you oversleep the switch to the cloud, you may be left behind in a few months or years. But of course there are understandable objections to the cloud hosting . We have gathered the advantages and disadvantages of cloud hosting for companies in numerous discussions with interested parties, competitors and colleagues. What speaks for the cloud, what speaks against it? Find out in our blog!

Cloud hosting for companies - 10 advantages and disadvantages at a glance

Flexibility

How much flexibility does the switch to the cloud really create? And isn't it risky to tie yourself to the cloud provider?

This speaks against the cloud: after signing the contract and switching to the cloud, you are bound to your cloud service provider and somewhat dependent on it. The technology stack also plays a role - once at Amazon AWS, the selection of other providers is small or the next switch is more complex. The type of cloud service should also be taken into account: the greater the role of the cloud provider, the greater the risk. Software-as-a-Service (SaaS) is 100% dependent, while infrastructure-as-a-service providers can be exchanged if the technology stack is the same (for example: Microsoft, VMware or CITRIX).

This speaks for the cloud: a cloud based on Infrastructure-as-a-Service can be moved relatively easily and converted back into a stationary network (although you have to plan and implement it carefully). Once the IT is virtualized, it can be expanded absolutely flexibly and bring more performance at peak times. The performance is performed by the cloud service - and is quickly taken into account for downtime - unlike you could ever with internal IT. If serious problems arise, switch to a provider with comparable services. So you can plan flexibly and without a long lead time.

Safety

Transferring the server and data to a cloud provider doesn't feel secure at first. But what about security compared to your own solutions?

This speaks against the cloud: An attack on the cloud provider endangers the security of your systems and data, and if the cloud provider has errors in the security concept, this affects your systems as well as all other customers of the cloud provider.

This speaks for the cloud: Public and private clouds are real bulwarks and much more secure than your own IT. Complex IT systems and logically separated networks significantly reduce many risks. All cloud hosters have their own security experts who only take care of securing the data and manage all countermeasures. Patches are imported at any time, updates are installed immediately and in general the cloud provider takes care of everything that would otherwise be left behind in everyday work - contractually regulated. Which company can say that about its own IT?

Price

Hardware prices are falling while system requirements are increasing. There is no significant change in IT investments for companies. Is cloud hosting worth it in comparison?

That speaks against the cloud: the first number in the estimate is usually surprisingly high. In principle, you could also drive cheaper with internal systems, but ...

That speaks for the cloud: ... but the cloud is considerably cheaper in terms of running costs compared to having your own data center if all factors are taken into account.

The costs not only include server hardware and licenses, but also the power supply, connection, personnel, security audits, installation, maintenance and support, suitable buildings (data centers) and much more. You usually pay for the all-round carefree service per month and you are only charged for what you actually use. You never have to worry about big purchases again. Many expensive investments are no longer necessary - the cloud is therefore financially worthwhile. This is a big advantage in cloud hosting.

Staff

Cloud hosting is not just outsourcing hardware. Above all, you also indirectly buy the necessary know-how for the operation of the IT infrastructure. What does this mean for your personnel structure?

This speaks against the cloud: If you have all the hardware and software in your own company, you have complete control over your resources. With an expert in charge of IT or a well-equipped IT department, you can individually tailor your technology and tailor it to the needs of the company.

This speaks for the cloud: Your IT staff can concentrate on the essentials when the hardware and the constant updating and backups are outsourced. The cloud offers more than enough options to adapt the offers and functions to your company's needs via IaaS. This allows your staff to concentrate on company-specific tasks and remains flexible in implementation. Ultimately, this means for you: more staff where it is closest to the value chain (process optimization, interfaces, ERP administration, etc.) and fewer staff in general operating expenses.

Connection and availability

Cloud vs. In-house IT infrastructure: this means that the distance between the company and its own servers is greater and is outside of its own catchment area. A risk?

This speaks against the cloud: For cloud computing to work in your company, there must be a stable and direct internet connection. When the internet is dead, nothing works anymore.

This speaks for the cloud: In the case of a cloud solution in your company, the contract specifies which accessibility is guaranteed and what the connection standard looks like. The guaranteed availability is usually 99.9% of the working time per year, with good providers 99.98% to 99.99%. If for any reason your cloud provider fails to secure this connection, the risk rests with them. Because there are contractual penalties that are due if the cloud is not available. The risk of failure on the customer side can also be significantly reduced via separate location connections. Especially with companies with multiple locations, there are significantly more arguments for cloud hosting than against it in terms of connection and availability.

Complexity

Compared to in-house IT, the cloud topic is almost brand new - and a correspondingly large number of "marketing terms" fly through the net, apparently without any definition. And now?

This speaks against the cloud: The first confrontation with cloud hosting can be difficult, especially for managers who are not very tech-savvy. All of the new terms and possibilities seem much more opaque than the good old company network. The company cannot avoid grappling with the possibilities and at least gaining a basic knowledge before starting such a project. Terms such as private cloud, public cloud, infrastructure-as-a-service and pay-as-you-go, as well as the allocation payment model are important for a decision.

That speaks for the cloud: Fast, uncomplicated, secure: Cloud hosting is a good alternative - especially if you have little technical know-how within the company. Because the cloud service provider takes care of all important aspects and regular security updates. The important points for you can then be contractually secured: availability, response times, resource quantities, backup plans, and additional service times. Detailed advice gives you exactly what you need - and you only pay for the service you use. Once you get started, cloud resources are really the better and more flexible option!

Everyday usability of cloud infrastructure

Can all common applications of medium-sized companies be operated in the cloud? And what happens in the event of an internet failure in the locations?

This speaks against the cloud: In principle, all applications can be operated in the cloud, a negative effect can arise if outdated software is used that is very network-intensive. In this case, a solution such as a terminal server or Citrix XenApp may have to be used to bring these to the locations with high performance. Of course, this increases the costs and the effort involved in moving.

When the internet is gone, the cloud dies too. Although the business impact in the event of an internet failure is already large, one thing is clear: the use of cloud servers makes the impact even clearer.

That speaks for the cloud: on the basis of Infrastructure-as-a-Service, you can run all of the applications that you have in the company today without any great effort during the migration. Thanks to the high-performance cloud infrastructure, everything runs better and faster after the changeover - and thanks to the high standards of a cloud provider, it is also safer. For larger locations, there is also the cloud connection via MPLS, here you get a direct line to the cloud resources, which are also available to the operator with fault clearance times of 4 hours.

The outsourcing of IT systems to Infrastructure-as-a-Service cloud services is a transfer of operational risk and management effort. You hand over many technical tasks to experts and can be sure through the contract that you will always be online. In everyday business, you have your head clear for the tasks that really count. Cloud hosting for medium-sized companies is definitely suitable for everyday use!

Scalability

The IT infrastructure in medium-sized companies must react more and more flexibly to the requirements. Planning periods of 36 months or more can hardly be considered.

This speaks against the cloud: Usually, certain quotas also have to be accepted from cloud providers. So there is no full flexibility, or only at an additional cost. Then you could argue that an internal server can also be easily expanded, right?

That speaks for the cloud: Not really. Because if you need a lot of computing power at peak times, you need them spontaneously. There is no time for concept creation, tendering, procurement, integration and testing. With a cloud, your connection and computing power automatically adapt to the needs from a resource inventory that already exists and does not have to be procured. This is also ideal for larger companies whose databases and ERP systems need a lot of power. Because with a cloud you can rent high-performance resources for which you would otherwise need your own, special and extremely expensive hardware.

Sustainability / Green IT

As is well known, the data centers of large cloud providers use as much electricity as entire small towns. Is that ecologically sensible and justifiable?

This speaks against the cloud: large servers require a lot of energy and have to run 24/7. This means that they consume a lot of electricity and need a lot of resources to keep up with the latest technology. A "power saving mode" cannot be implemented in such data centers.

This speaks for the cloud: a modern bus and an older car with four seats consume approximately the same amount of gasoline and emit a similar amount of pollutants. In return, the bus transports a lot more people.

The situation is similar with server technology: A large cloud server costs less electricity and energy overall than hundreds or thousands of small servers that are located individually in the company. This means that switching to the cloud in terms of sustainability is a point for a clear conscience. In addition, many providers rely on 100% green electricity, for example - not a matter of course for a medium-sized company.

Future

Where is the trend going? Taking into account the current development in IT, you should take a critical look at your own IT infrastructure, because outdated systems often generate high costs in operation and the risk of failure increases. So, are cloud resources the way to go?

This speaks against the cloud: little.

This speaks for the cloud: everything! With a corporate cloud, you are flexible and can face the challenges of the future with ease. The responsibility for the technology lies in the hands of your cloud hosting service provider, who takes over the investment in constantly new computer systems with Infrastructure-as-a-Service. The management effort of IT technology is thus outsourced and is in competent hands. Your staff focuses on process optimization, creating interfaces and integrating innovative applications to give your company a competitive advantage. So you are well prepared for the future!

THE AMAZON EC2

The Amazon EC2 service provides computing resources performed in a virtual environment and all managed in cloud computing. The term EC2 of the name derives from the concept of Elastic Compute Cloud. In fact, it will be possible to take advantage not only of a fixed power established a priori but of an elastic power, which as you can guess from the name is a type of computational power that adapts to realtime needs. Therefore it grows when we need it and decreases when not we use it.

Amazon EC2 belongs to the IAAS (Infrastructure as a service) level that provides basic virtual resources, exactly as if they were hardware components, so we will have full control over all the operations we can perform, we can install operating systems and all the that we need. The downside is that all maintenance, updating, safety and control operations will be our responsibility and therefore will need a system figure.

Introduction

The elastic feature of the service and the direct integration with all the other AWS makes this environment one of the most used in cloud computing besides the fact that it can save a lot of money compared to a classic infrastructure. It is no coincidence that many large companies, even with important names, have scaled down the corporate data centres by eliminating many hardware resources in favour of cloud computing services.

The Amazon EC2 service is very powerful but also very complex. So we will make sure that it is presented on different articles, to make more specific tutorials at the end and discover the most hidden details. We will start with the explanation of the elastic concept, with the costs of the service, we will explain the purchase options, the types of instances, the dashboard, the AMI, the authorizations, EBS, the balancing, the auto-scaling, etc., etc.

In short, if you want to know this service well, you will have to be patient because it is not enough to read only this article :) As regards the information of all the other services that can be integrated with Amazon EC2 you can find them in our general guide, if you prefer the video format, on our youtube channel. Anything you don't find in our resources you can always discuss it in the community.

Elasticity

Whenever I find myself explaining this concept, I always try to solve by giving a practical example. So let's take the case of a company that sells products on the internet and receives a number of orders every day. It is certain that the number of orders that will be received will not always be the same every day, but there will be periods where sales can drop and others where they can triple, for example, think of the Christmas periods or the days that are in the middle of a commercial campaign.

As you can see from this graph, to solve the problem in the traditional way, the company will have to buy a server that allows it to overcome the requests generated in the highest period of the year and therefore keep unused resources for the rest of the period, which of course also means economic waste. Unfortunately, although this detail can be accepted, another important aspect is not resolved.

What happens if sales exceed expectations, and I need additional power? In a classic structure, a disservice would be generated; in fact, the time needed to scale the current resources would not be fast enough to avoid losing sales. I can assure you that the number of realities that have reached this point is many more than we can imagine, there have been companies that in moments of great unexpected success have found themselves with web servers and related applications in a status error 500 for reaching the maximum limit of allowed connections.

Scalability

Starting from an established computational power, it is possible to decrease or increase the necessary resources in two ways: one called vertical scalability and the other horizontal scalability. In the first case we do nothing but replace on the fly a virtual server of a certain power with an even more powerful one, while in the second case we add a new server or even more than one and create a balanced traffic environment.

In vertical scalability, we have an advantage of the simplicity of action, but on the other hand, we have a small downtime to change servers and more importantly there is a limit represented by the most powerful server that we can buy. In fact, if we reach this level, we would no longer have a further scalability solution.

In horizontal scalability we have a theoretically infinite scalability limit, in the sense that we can always add a new server as much as this is necessary, it is also obvious that the configuration of this environment is much more complex than vertical scalability, but it is certainly the most used in the internet environment.

I personally use both ways; it depends on the environment I find myself configuring. The vertical scalability is fine when you have to make available computational resources to a company for well-defined processes or when there are applications that can not be changed for an environment horizontal. As for internet applications, I always try to use horizontal scalability, excluding the conditions in which the ERP software is not suitable for this type of activity.

Costs

The costs of the Amazon EC2 service are based on the hourly use of the instances, which have different characteristics of power, memory and bandwidth. On the official page, you will always find updated values; in fact, they change very frequently and fortunately, always on the downside. The method called "pay-to-use" is based on the fact of paying only the resources that are used and optimizing costs as much as possible according to real needs.

InstanceCPURAMNowDayYear

Instance	CPU	RAM	Now	Day	Year
t2.micro	1	1.0 GB	$ 0.013	$ 0.312	$ 113.88
t2.medium	2	4.0 GB	$ 0.052	$ 1.288	$ 455.52
m3.large	2	7.5 GB	$ 0.140	$ 3,360	$ 1,226.40
m3.xlarge	4	15.0 GB	$ 0.280	$ 6,720	$ 2,452.80

In this table, I have listed only a few instances; in reality, there are many others that we will analyze calmly in the next chapters. Prices may change slightly depending on the geographical region they belong to, for example, an EC2 instance in Europe costs a little more than launch on the USA region.

Also do not pay much attention to the annual cost column, as we are talking about on-demand instances. Therefore they are taken on request as needed. If you need servers that work all day without stopping, you need to analyze the reserved instances on which you also save 40/50% compared to the on-demand table. In this case, you have to pay an advance payment and get a lower hourly cost.

InstanceCPURAMAdvanceNowYearTotal

Instance	CPU	RAM	Advance	Now	Year	Total
t2.micro	1	1.0 GB	$ 51	$ 0.003	$ 26.28	$ 77.88
t2.medium	2	4.0 GB	$ 204	$ 0.012	$ 105.12	$ 309.12
m3.large	2	7.5 GB	$ 443	$ 0.037	$ 324.12	$ 767.12
m3.xlarge	4	15.0 GB	$ 886	$ 0.047	$ 411.72	$ 1,297.72

As you can see with the reserved you also save 50%, in reality there are different types of reserved, based on the constant use of resources. I used the reserved Heavy in this table , but there are also Light and Medium

For more detailed information on the relationship between the cost and the elastic nature of the service, I recommend reading an article that I had dedicated to Amazon EC2 costs and entitled "Amazon EC2 how to calculate costs on Elastic Compute Cloud".

Purchase options

The available options are on-demand, reserved and spot. If nothing is specified, an on-demand instance will be used, which provides only the hourly cost and no particular limit on the use. I also want to remember that the type of purchase does not affect the type of instance; these remain technically always the same; only the billing method applied changes.

On-Demand: instances that allow you to pay for processing capacity hour by hour, without long-term commitments. This avoids the complexity of planning, purchasing and maintaining hardware and transforms what are commonly high costs into much smaller variable costs. (use in the short term).

Reserved: there are instances that require constant use of resources over time; there are three types of reserved: Heavy, Light and Medium. Each of these is based on how much time you use the resources in the year if, for example, you have a web server access 24 hours a day obviously you have to select the Heavy which will give you maximum savings.

Spot: in these types of requests, you pay the price established by a mechanism similar to the exchange, based on supply and demand. We must specify the maximum price we are willing to pay, the geographical region and the area of availability. If the current price is lower or equal to our request, we will have an instance running.

Type of instances

The service offers a wide range of instances optimized for different use cases. The instances include various combinations of CPU, memory, storage and networking capabilities and offer the flexibility to choose the appropriate mix of resources to suit our applications better. Each instance type includes different sizes, allowing you to scale resources based on the needs of our workload.

Instances (T2): they have been designed for workloads that do not use the entire CPU or that do not make continuous use of it, but need to use it from time to time. The benchmark for performance CPU and the ability to go beyond this value (burst) are regulated by the receivables of CPUs (CPU Credits).

Instances (M3): this family is designed for an optimization that regards memory and network resources. These instances are recommended for many applications, for example, for small databases or software such as SAP and Sharepoint. For the M3, Intel Xeon E5-2670 processors and SSD internal disks are used to obtain excellent performance.

Instances (C3): they have been designed to obtain CPU performance, ideal for applications that make extensive use of computing. These instances are suitable for processing engineering programs, distributed analysis, video encoding, etc. Intel Xeon E5-2670 processors and internal high-performance SSD disks are used.

Instances (R3): they are optimized for applications that require a lot of RAM and lower the standard cost per GB of memory. They are suitable for high-performance databases, cache systems and for developers in Enterprise environments. Intel Xeon E5-2670 processors and high-performance SSD internal disks are used.

Instances (G2): this family is designed for graphic environments and for particular streaming software and video encoding. High-performance NVIDIA GPU with 1,536 CUDA cores and 4GB of video memory. Support for low-latency frame capture and encoding. Intel Xeon E5-2670 processors and high-performance SSD internal disks are used.

Instances (I2): this family has been designed to obtain large quantities of storage, these instances can be used for NoSQL databases such as Cassandra or MongoDB, data warehousing, Hadoop and cluster file systems. Obviously, the instances are equipped with very fast SSD disks that make the machine perform.

A MANUAL FOR THE USE OF S3, AWS GLUE AND ATHENA

If you work with large amounts of data on a local computer, you will soon be confronted with a lack of extra memory and storage, overheating of the processor, long waiting times, etc. Nowadays, more and more companies, institutions or projects are offering 'big data'. Create that is no longer easy to analyze with your local computer. This is one of many other reasons why cloud services have increased exponentially in popularity in recent years. By storing this big data on servers in the cloud, you keep the local computer storage free. Also, the calculations or processes that can be performed by hireable 'super' computers within the cloud will be considerably faster than if they were executed locally.

The reason I started working in the cloud was that I had to quickly extract specific subsets for a job from a massive set of traffic data (15TB), and then continue working with it locally. With the help of various services in the cloud, this is easy, fast and relatively inexpensive. Of the different cloud providers, I automatically rolled into Amazon Web Services (AWS), and I noticed that relatively little is still being worked in the cloud in my environment.

These services are 'S3' (Simple Storage Server) for storage, 'AWS Glue' for indexing all data, and 'Athena' as an interactive SQL query service. The function, the benefits and the use of these services will be discussed in more detail.

You can create an AWS account for free and follow the steps of this blog directly. Perhaps useful if you already want to scale up to the cloud and, for example, also want to run queries within large data sets.

"THE CLOUD"

There are many different cloud providers, one with more services than the other. In 2019, AWS was the market leader with the most users worldwide. This can perhaps be explained by the fact that AWS currently has the most extensive range of services. However, Azure from Microsoft has gained enormously in popularity in recent years. Like AWS, Azure is user-friendly and has many similar services compared to AWS. Azure, like other cloud providers, will probably equal AWS in the near future. By then, the difference will probably only be in the prices. Before choosing a cloud provider, it is always good to first properly identify which cloud best fits the work you want to perform. Since many cloud providers offer multiple matching services, it will generally not matter much which cloud you choose. Of course, this does matter if your goal is very specific.

This blog will therefore only delve further into AWS, although I certainly recommend that you also look at other cloud providers.

An example of a selection from the various cloud providers and the relationships in use.

AMAZON WEB SERVICES (AWS)

S3, AWS Glue, Athena

AWS has been around since 2006 and offers more than 160 services after 13 years. You probably won't need them all, but it indicates that a lot is possible. The various services include computing, storage, database, media services, machine learning, AR & VR, analytics, migration & transfer and much more. AWS is a 'pay-as-you-go' system, which means that you only pay when you actually use the services. This keeps the costs for the user as low and clear as possible.

If you don't have an AWS account yet, but you want to follow the steps in this blog directly, go to https://aws.amazon.com (or https://aws.amazon.com/premiumsupport/knowledge -center/create) -and-activate-aws account /). Creating an account is free, although having an AWS account is not necessary to follow the rest of this blog! It also serves as general information about the services that will be explained.

The AWS main page looks like this:

On this page, you can immediately see a clear overview of all services that AWS offers under the heading 'All services', with the recently used services as a shortcut above them.

At the top of the 'Services' tab, you can also quickly search for the desired service.

Also important is the location of the servers in which you work, which in this example is on 'Frankfurt'.

AWS has servers spread around the world, and you can, for example, store your data in different locations or run your APIs on different servers. If one server is down, you can switch to another quickly. This means that if you do everything on one server and this server gets problems, then there is nothing else to do than wait until the server does it again. Spread can somewhat benefit prevention.

S3

The Simple Storage Service is the most popular service that AWS offers. It is a service where you can store data in 'buckets', or folders in the AWS environment. Here you can store huge amounts of data and also get started right away since the data is already in the AWS environment.

This environment looks like this:

The image below shows the content of a new bucket named 'blog-example-bucket'. Here you can easily upload files and create folders within the bucket.

However, it is even easier and more stable to upload files to or download from a bucket, or exchange files between buckets via your terminal. To do this, first configure your AWS account:

In terminal:

- Type: Aws configure
- Enter your AWS Access Key ID
- Give your AWS Secret Access Key
- Specify the desired default region name. If this is already on 'EU-central-1', then this can stay that way.
- Specify the desired default output format. If this is set to 'None', then this can also remain the case.

Example:

If you enter the following in terminal you copy the entire contents of your relevant folder to, for example, the new 'blog-example-bucket' S3 bucket:

- aws s3 cp / user / path s3: // blog-example-bucket / --recursive
- ('–Recursive' means that the command is repeated for each file in the selected folder.)

AWS GLUE

With the help of AWS Glue, you can transform your data, which is stored in S3 buckets for example, and then analyze it. This service is also called an 'extract, transform, and load' (ETL) service. Essentially you can index data so that it can act as a virtual SQL database. This virtual SQL database can, in turn, be queried by Athena; a service that will be explained further in this blog.

Creating such a virtual SQL database is done through a crawler. This crawler extracts and transforms the data, creates a table and puts this table in a database. The tables of the databases can be requested in Athena.

AWS Glue looks like this:

Creating a crawler:

Click 'Add crawler.'

Give the crawler a name. (You can tag the crawler, security or classifiers here, but this is not necessary.) In this example, the crawler is called "blog-example-crawler." Click 'Next'.

At 'Crawler source type' choose 'Datastores'. Click 'Next'.

Then choose the data that the crawler will use. The settings in this example are as follows:

- Choose a data store: S3
- Crawl data in Specified path in my account
- Include path: s3: // blog-example-bucket

Click 'Next'.

Now you can add another data store, for example, other buckets, to the crawler. In this example, we stick to the 'blog-example-bucket' bucket, so click on 'No' and then 'Next'.

I give the IAM role the same name as what I called the crawler ('blog-example-bucket') to keep the overview. Of course, this can be all, as long as you can find it later. Then click 'Next'.

In this step ('Schedule'), you can set when you want to run the crawler. This can be 'on-demand' or periodic. Please note: the costs can easily add up if you have the crawler run periodically, especially if you forget to switch it off if it is no longer needed. In this example, it is on 'Run On Demand'. Click 'Next'.

We have now arrived at the 'Output' step. If all goes well, there will be no database at 'Database' that you can choose, as they have not yet been created. Select 'Add database'; in this example, I call the database 'blog-example-database'. No further options are required, but you can see what the optional adjustments do exactly. Then click 'Next'.

This is a final check before you start creating the crawler. Once everything is correct click 'Finish'.

The result looks like this:

When there is data in the bucket that the crawler is over and you click on 'Run crawler', the entire contents of this bucket will be indexed in one table. You can find this table under the 'Tables' tab on the left side of the menu.

To summarize: You have now created a crawler that has merged all files in a specific S3 bucket into one large table, after which this table is stored in a created database.

ATHENA

Athena is an interactive SQL query service that is an excellent tool for working with large amounts of data. As mentioned earlier, you can request the tables that were created with the AWS Glue crawlers.

Athena looks like this:

First check which server you are on. This is indicated at the top right (in the image it is on 'Ohio'). When you first open Athena, it may just be that it is set to a different server than the one you were working with AWS Glue. As long as the servers in which you work with Athena and where your databases (made with AWS Glue) are stored, do not match, it is therefore not possible to request these databases, and therefore the tables, in Athena.

In the menu on the left, you can select the desired database that you have created with AWS Glue, after which the tables that appear in this database will appear.

To view the table quickly, do the following:

- Click on the three dots behind the table that you have created that you want to see.
- Click 'Preview table'.
- The query that runs automatically then looks like this:
- SELECT * FROM "database_name". "Table_name" limit 10;

Incidentally, it is not required to select the correct database in the left menu to work in it. Create your query and state after the statement "FROM" from which database you want which table. So: FROM "database_name". "Table_name"

Once the query has been executed, the result can be seen below. With the icon which is circled in red in the example below, the result of the query can be directly downloaded as a .csv file.

You can easily save the created query and call it up later to work on.

Press 'Save as' and your saved queries can be found at the top of the menu, under the 'Saved Queries' heading.

Athena also automatically keeps a record of the history of your queries. If you have accidentally deleted part of a query, you can easily find it again in the same menu under the 'History' heading.

AMAZON EC2 HOW TO CALCULATE COSTS ON ELASTIC COMPUTE CLOUD

The question regarding the costs of the Amazon EC2 service is certainly one of the most frequent in the AWS sector. The main reason is related to the fact that not being a fixed cost on a monthly or annual basis; this creates some perplexities, in fact, it is not possible, as for other internet services, such as hosting services, to have a fixed annual price and to obtain against a well-defined package of services.

Amazon, for the provision of its services in the cloud, uses the payment technique called " pay-as-you-use" which translated means "pay only for what you use".

Initially, wanting to purchase services whose costs must be calculated with formulas and despite having unpredictable factors such as traffic, can rightly lead to insecurities, however, if we analyze well the reason for this choice we will immediately realize how much it is more flexible than a fixed-cost service.

Amazon EC2 is not a hosting or dedicated server service, the EC2 service is much more and allows us to buy quantities of processing in a cloud system for the time and power we need, that then with this technique we can configure a working and active web server 24H24 this is only a single aspect of the dozens of possibilities made available.

Cost calculation on EC2

To calculate the costs of a virtual server you have to go to the EC2 Pricing section and look for the "geographical area" you want to work on, in fact, the costs of the data centre in Ireland are different from those in Virginia in the United States. Once you have selected the region, you will see a table divided by the required computing power and the operating system to be installed. In fact, if we install Linux, we will have a lower price than Windows, as we don't have to pay the M $ license.

Some EC2 instancesPrice calculationAnnual

Linux M1.Micro	(0.020 hour) x 24 x 365	$ 175
Linux M1.Small	(0.047 hour) x 24 x 365	$ 412
Linux M3.Medium	(0.077 hour) x 24 x 365	$ 675
Linux M3.Large	(0.154 hour) x 24 x 365	$ 1,349

In the example that I have reported, I have indicated the prices of the service with reference to an annual cost to give a rough idea, in reality, these rates should be used only when a virtual server is requested for a certain period, for example, a few hours, a week or month. If you need intensive activity, you need the reserved.

In fact, if I have a different need, as in the case of a web server active 24H24 for the whole year, I have to refer to the reserved instances. With this type of instance, you pay one-off based on the power required and the hourly rate is much lower, I bring you the example of before showing you the savings that can be obtained.

Some EC2 instancesPrice calculationAnnualAdvanceTotal

		Annual	Advance	Total
Linux M1.Micro	(0.008 hour) x 24 x 365	$ 70	$ 62	$ 132
Linux M1.Small	(0.016 hour) x 24 x 365	$ 140	$ 123	$ 263
Linux M3.Medium	(0.028 hour) x 24 x 365	$ 245	$ 222	$ 467
Linux M3.Large	(0.057 hour) x 24 x 365	$ 499	$ 443	$ 942

Attention : The prices shown change continuously, obviously over time they become lower and lower, so do not take these tables only as an example to calculate the annual price of your application. Always see on EC2 Pricing .

Pay-to-use for development environments

There are cases where together with the production servers there are development servers, these servers are not always used, but only during the periods of software development or for any tests before being put into production. This feature forces the company to purchase a server that entails double costs, related to licenses, hardware maintenance, system configuration, network configurations, etc.

In short, a large amount of money spent to have something available all year round when only part of it is actually used. If instead of this solution the one proposed by Amazon were adopted, we will pay the rent of a server only for a month or two, in this way the savings are significant. I personally have seen several customers spend 8/10 thousand euros for huge development servers that have been inside the data centres for months to collect dust waiting for test needs.

Not to mention that on the cloud it is possible to have infinite development environments, as we could duplicate the production server and try further modifications on another server equal to the first and this maybe only for a few hours — very useful and interesting but prohibitive possibilities in the classic networking environment.

Pay-to-use for research processing

Many times the required processing has a very specific feature, they need power, but for a short time. In these cases, the savings can be very high; in fact, without this possibility, it would be necessary to buy very expensive resources and servers to use them only sometimes. A huge waste of resources.

Instead with the "pay-to-use" method, it is possible to rent 100/200 servers or even more for parallel processing only for a few hours or days, the time necessary to run the scientific algorithm which will then be the work base for the next few months. It is not difficult to understand that in these cases, the difference would not be only the economic aspect, but we think about how many management problems are spared to the team itself.

Try the software and operating systems

Sometimes we may need to try a new operating system to test the functioning of an application and see if there may be problems with a malfunction before an update. In the traditional environment, this would be very expensive, as we need to duplicate resources.

In the cloud environment, instead, just start an EC2 instance with the operating system to be tested, install our software, do all the necessary tests and write a working report. All this without buying any hardware and avoiding all the problems of system configuration and implementation of the case. From personal experience, I assure you that there have been cases where I was able to try the software with a different operating system even in a few hours with a cost of 3/4 euro.

Another interesting case was to do a test on WordPress software for a very popular site, which did not want to risk with an update to be faced with problems to solve. In this case, I duplicated the server image on a second server, on which I performed the update that the client was able to try. The server was online for two days at the cost of around € 10.

Pay power only when needed

This is perhaps the clearest aspect of why " paying for what you use " can be very beneficial. Take for example a portal that has an average of more or less consistent visits on a monthly basis during the year, but in two months of the year, which could, for example, be the Christmas holidays and the first summer month, it must face a more accesses and page views than the annual average.

The machine will have to have a power equal to its maximum stress. Therefore it would be necessary to buy or rent a server that for only two months a year will be able to use its power, while for the remaining 10 months it will only be a wasted cost.

In the cloud world of Amazon EC2, this does not happen; for this reason, it is called Elastic Compute, in fact, we can pay for 10 months the necessary power and only for the two exceptional months we will pay extra for the additional power.

General warning of costs

The following guide was written for information purposes with the aim of explaining the characteristics of " pay-to-use " and the method of calculating costs. In any case, if you want to make an exact cost analysis for your environment, always use the amazon tables that you find on the official website.

Amazon EC2 a tutorial to use the service

Use of the service

As we have done for other services, we should analyze all the options in the dashboard menu and then see how to use them one by one. So, as always, first, we select the geographic region we want to use and then the EC2 service, once this is done, we should get this screen:

The dashboard is split into several sections; the first indicates the main menu with all the components that can be found in the service with the configuration parameters. In the central part, we find an overview of active resources, the key to start a new instance and the general status of the service in the geographical region. In the right sidebar, we find links to various information and official documentation.

(1) Main menu: this is the section in which we find all the options related to the service and the various components that we can configure. We will analyze this

menu better in the next chapter, and we will see together each component related to the service.

(2) Resources: in this section, it is possible to have an overview of the resources that have been started in the EC2 environment. For example, the running instances, the number of active volumes, the access keys, the number of public IPs, snapshots etc. etc.

(3) Start instance: here you find the blue button to start a new EC2 instance; in reality, this possibility will be present in different parts of the console. In fact, we can start a new instance from the instance menu or from the AMI menu.

(4) Service status: in this section, you can check the general status of the Amazon EC2 service within the selected region. So if you have problems with some instances, always remember to check the dashboard first.

(5) Information: on the side sidebar we find links to very useful external resources, for example, documentation, discussion forum and marketplace to search for pre-packaged solutions to be launched in the EC2 environment.

Main menu

The main menu that we find on the service page provides us with different sections that identify the various components of the service; we find the general section, the management of instances, the AMI images, the storage volumes, the section dedicated to security and networking and advanced services such as autoscaling. For a complete presentation, we try to analyze each point:

EC2 Dashboard: through this option, it is possible to see the screen of the previous chapter which is started even when selecting the EC2 service from the main menu, useful for seeing the resources used or looking for additional information.

Events: by selecting this option, you can check all the events that have been created with reference to EC2 instances. Events can be generated via status check or via alarms defined in the Amazon CloudWatch service.

Tags: all the resources present in Amazon EC2 have the possibility of associating a Name type TAG that can be useful for identifying the resource and the type of use that we had decided for the resource itself. In this screen, it will be possible to see the number of resources associated with a given TAG and check its operation.

Reports: in this section, it is possible to activate or view very detailed reports concerning the use of EC2 resources and their billing. You can choose the statistics that relate to on-demand or confidential instances. In this way, we can analyze statistics that allow us to choose the purchase options correctly and obtain savings on the cost of the service.

Limits: When you open a new account in Amazon AWS, you can immediately use all the services that you need to try. But it is good to know that there are limits on the number of resources that can be used simultaneously. The existence of this limit serves to prevent the creation of fake accounts that can only be used to launch an infinite number of resources. Obviously, if these limits are low for a genuine account, just request an increase.

Instances: with this option, it is possible to view the list of active EC2 instances and perform various operations, such as stopping, reboot, creation of AMI, management of connected disks, etc. etc. On each instance, you can view the configuration options that were used for startup and security auditing. Obviously, it is also possible to launch a new instance, an operation that we will analyze later.

Spot Request: in this section, you can configure a spot instance request that we presented in the previous Amazon EC2 article introduction. In any case, these are instances that will be launched only when the market price is equal to or less than the maximum price that we are willing to pay.

Reserved Instances: when we start an instance, the purchase option called on-demand is used, where we pay a fixed fee for each hour of use. If we need to use an instance for a long time, it is possible to buy some reserved ones which allow us to save money with an advance payment.

AMIs: in this section, we find the AMI (Amazon Machine Image) which contain the virtual images that are used by the instances that we will launch. Each image can contain a different operating system, specific configurations, the software already installed and configured in our application environment and ready for use.

Bundle Tasks: here you can find the list of jobs that are creating AMI to be used as store-backed in Windows environment. Linux ones are more immediate and don't need to go through this type of processing.

Volumes: with this option, we can manage and view all the mechanical and SSD disks connected to our instances, both active and terminated. Volumes like instances can only exist in an availability zone, so for added security, it is best to create backup snapshots periodically.

Snapshots: they are mirror copies of the corresponding volumes, they are also used by the AMI to create the volumes to be attached to the instances that will be started. Unlike volumes, snapshots are stored at the geographical region level and therefore, as the data stored on S3 are redundant due to their architectural nature.

Security Groups: for each instance, we can associate a security group that is used to control the protocols and ports enabled by the virtual server to respond. If we are working in Amazon VPC, it is possible to define rules both at the level of subnets and ACL on the security group, which intervenes subsequently.

Elastic IPs: if we are to release a public application on the internet, we must have a static IP address to use every time we start our instance. In this section, we can reserve IP addresses and associate them with our account for an indefinite period. We can use these addresses with Amazon Route 53.

Placement Groups: is a grouping of instances within a single availability zone. Using these groups allows applications to participate in a 10 Gbps low latency network.

Load Balancers: in this section, it is possible to configure the service for the division of the workload between different instances running the same application. We saw this concept in the introductory article, where we talked about horizontal scalability and the characteristics that must be known for its application.

Key Pairs: the default connection for an active instance is to use the SSH protocol with an RSA key that is generated by the Amazon service. Through this menu, you can create new keys or delete existing ones. The key can be downloaded only during the creation phase; if you lose it for any reason, the only way to solve it is to create a new one and associate it with the instance.

Network Interfaces: when we start a new EC2 instance in a VPC environment, it is possible to associate network

115

interfaces to which to assign IP addresses. Through this section, it is possible to list the active interfaces, change the network characteristics or create new interfaces for the active instances or those still to be started.

Auto Scaling: With this option, it is possible to define automatic rules to add virtual servers to our application. In any case, this option will be covered in the next article and will cover advanced functions.

Start our instance

To start a new instance, we must have several things: first, an AMI that contains the operating system and the software we need, but since it is our first instance and we don't have an AMI yet, we will use a default one which then it can be stored in our account privately. We also need an SSH connection key and a security group to enable access ports.

(1) Creating a key: go to the Key pairs menu and select the blue button from the main menu " Create Key Pair ", indicate a name and confirm. An automatic download of the key will be performed at our local station. Keep it aside from that we will use it with the SSH client to connect to the instance once started.

(2) Security Group: we always go to the specific menu called security groups and also create a new security group with the name Group / SEC. In the configuration screen, we must also specify a description, select a default VPC and insert the ports enabled to connect with the instance itself.

(3) Start an instance: we are finally ready to start an instance, since we do not have our own AMI, at the moment we will select a default one present in the list of Amazon Web Services and then we will modify it according to our needs. First, we go to the Instances menu and select " Launch Instance ".

As you can see, you have several AMI ready for use on which you can choose different operating systems and architectures. If you are using the free trial offer called " Free tier ", you must select only the AMI that contains this wording. Otherwise, you will be charged for the on-demand costs of the application. In this example, I will select the AMI called Ubuntu Server 14.04 LTS (HVM) SSD Volume Type.

Once the AMI has been selected, we move on to the choice of the type of instance, which, as we saw in the previous article, represents the characteristics of the server to be started, such as the CPU, RAM memory, internal disks, etc.

For testing purposes, the instance (t2.micro) or also (t2.small) is fine for slightly heavier applications. At this point, we select the type of instance and press the " Configure Instance Details " button for the different configurations. The following screen is the most important of all, and you need to know the required parameters well.

Number of instances: indicates the number of instances to be started at the same time with the configuration we are preparing. Normally you can use this option to manage manual scalability and therefore without Auto Scaling or start the first series of servers after a global stop for a general configuration change.

Purchase option: we can indicate if the instance is a spot type, it is not necessary to do it for reserved instances, in fact, these would be applied automatically if the instance will be started in the default availability zone. At the moment we leave the default and launch an on-demand instance, later we will see better this aspect.

Network: we must select a VPC network in which to run this instance, once there was also an area dedicated to

EC2 without having to use VPC, this possibility has remained with the old accounts but has been eliminated by the new ones. So VPC has become mandatory. Read our article on VPC for more information.

Subnet: within a VPC configuration there are subnets, both public and private, in this tutorial, we will select a public subnet so that we can test after starting the instance via the standard internet connection.

Public IP: indicates whether a public IP address should be assigned during startup. If we have to use the Elastic IP of our account, we can do without this option, but if we have to start an instance and have public access immediately, we must enable the option. In our case, we select (enable).

IAM Role: the role is a very important aspect of EC2 security, in fact, if our applications need to use other services, for example, S3 to make backups or Amazon SES to send mail, we should specify in our scripts the login credentials. With the roles, it is the instance itself the guarantee, and the allowed accesses are defined in the role itself. This significantly increases security.

Shutdown behaviour: indicates the action performed on the physical instance when the shutdown command is specified at the operating system level. Council to always use the stop value instead of that of (terminate) for a series of implications that we will see in the articles dedicated to Amazon EC2 that concern the more advanced aspects.

Termination protection: activating this protection it is not possible to terminate the instance from the console or via API if protection is not deactivated first.

Monitoring: indicates whether to activate advanced data collection concerning the use of resources related to the EC2 instance. Normally the statistics are collected with a series of 5 minutes; if we activate this option, we will go down to the level of one minute.

Tenancy: with this option, you can run the instance on dedicated hardware. This is ideal in corporate policies or industry regulations that require physical and not just virtual isolation from instances of other customers. If you select this type of hardware, you will have additional costs, read the documentation carefully.

Now that we have clarified the options indicated, we can move to the storage screen where you can select the hard disks that we want to hook to our instance, each type of instance always has a pre-defined disk, and we can use only that, if the need were different we could add later.

The next steps are the management of the tags, which we can leave out at the moment, and the configuration of the security group, which consists in choosing the group created at the beginning of this chapter before starting the instance. Once this step is finished, we will also be asked for the access key, and finally, the instance will be started.

SSH connection

Once our instance is ready, we can connect to it and make all the configurations and changes that we need to install our application. Just go to the " Instances " menu, select the instance and press the Connect button. We will see a pop-up window with the data concerning access. Obviously, the key must be present on our PC.

We execute these instructions on our terminal and connect to the instance. If we don't use a command line, we can download the SSH Putty client and enter the connection parameters in the session configuration.

Using Putty, remember that the key has to be converted. See the official documentation.

If we have done the steps correctly, we should connect to our instance and be in the Linux terminal session. Once inside, we can execute any command without any limit since in EC2, we have full control of our instance, and we can add any software we need.

New software installation

Now that we have control of our instance, we can try to update the operating system and maybe install new software such as Apache, PHP and MySQL.

pets HTTP and HTTPS requests (remember the security group?) We can try to make a request with our favourite browser to the IP address with which we connected in SSH.

If we have done everything correctly, this should be the result page with apache just installed. Of course, add any tests you normally run on a traditional server and check the result.

Creating an AMI

Perhaps the time has come to create an image that contains our new updated operating system and the software that we have installed for the needs required by our application. Also because it would not be nice to start from the default AMI and reinstall everything every time :) The solution to the problem is very simple, just create a (private) AMI starting from our active instance.

To do this, we have to go to (instances) and select our desired instance. With the right mouse button, a drop-down menu appears where you can find a menu item called " Create Image ", select this item and insert the required fields such as name, description and characteristics of the volume.

Once the creation of an AMI has been requested, it will be necessary to wait a few minutes before the operation is completed. To check the progress, just go to the snapshots section and then to the AMI section. You will find a progress bar next to the resource, which should indicate the current percentage.

AMAZON EC2 ADVANCED WITH LOAD BALANCING AND AUTO SCALING.

Amazon SQS is a queuing system that allows applications, in a fast and reliable way, to queue messages to exchange among themselves in an asynchronous way, each message, in turn, can generate other more specific processing. This system allows you to create highly scalable environments and convert complex applications into several simpler and independent processing units.

To understand each other we can imagine any scenario, for example, we have a web procedure that receives requests for video uploads, this application instead of converting the video and generating the corresponding cover images, only queues a message. This, in turn, will be processed by a different component, perhaps even on a different server, which will save time for the main application which in turn does not have to wait for the complete cycle to process the next upload request.

Introduction

Using Amazon SQS, it is possible to separate the components of an application so that they can function independently. This means that the queue solves problems that can arise when the component that produces the data produces more work than the receiving component can process. Or if the producer and consumer are not continuously connected to the network.

A single queue can be used by many components of distributed applications without the need for these components to coordinate with each other.

One of the resulting compromises is that Amazon SQS does not guarantee first in, first out in the delivery of messages. For many distributed applications, each message has its own autonomy, and since all messages are delivered, the order is no longer important. If your system requires that the order must be respected, you can insert sequence information within each message so that you can reorder them through the application when the queue returns them.

Main functions

This is the list of features that are available in the Amazon SQS service :

Redundant infrastructure: guarantees message delivery at least once, concurrent access and high availability for sending and retrieving messages.

Multiple writers and readers: multiple parties can send and receive messages at the same time. Amazon SQS blocks messages during their processing.

Configurable settings for queue: the queues do not necessarily have to be the same; for example, a queue can be optimized for a type of message that requires more processing time than others.

Variable message size: messages can reach a maximum size of 262.144 bytes (256KB). For messages larger than 256 KB, you can use Amazon S3 to store the message content and use Amazon SQS to keep the pointer to Amazon S3 or the subject. Alternatively, you can divide the message into smaller parts.

Access control: it is possible to manage the permissions on who can send the message to the queue and on who is authorized to receive the message from the queue.

Delay queues: it is set to define the delay time for sending all the messages that have been inserted. If this value is changed, the new value will only take effect for messages that will be queued after the change.

Scalable environment

Using an application based on Amazon SQS not only allows you to simplify the main application and an improvement in overall performance but also allows you to obtain a highly scalable environment. For example, let's take a crawl software used by a search engine, not only is it a complex project that concerns the storage algorithms but it is also for what concerns the dynamics for the collection of information, in this case, queue management is a good solution.

In this example, starting from the left, we have the pages present on the internet that are read by a series of servers, the latter at each reading instead of analyzing the page they send the function to another process with a message, which always with a series of servers provides a more specific sorting, for example sending request messages on queues for the analysis of HTML content, specific queues for images, PDF documents etc. These queues are processed by software that stores a result on a common database. In this way, each component lives its own life and is not influenced by the speed of the others.

Property

A queue can be empty if no messages have been sent to it or if all the messages within it have been deleted. Each queue must be given a name; a queue can be cancelled at any time, full or empty. Amazon SQS can delete a queue without warning if one of the following actions is not found for at least 30 consecutive days: SendMessage, ReceiveMessage, DeleteMessage, GetQueueAttributes, SetQueueAttributes, AddPermission and RemovePermission.

Important: This is a violation of Amazon SQS 's intended use if you repeatedly create queues and then leave them inactive, or if you store excessive amounts of data in the queues. In fact, the queues are designed to process messages as soon as possible and not to store permanent information.

At-Least-Once Delivery: Amazon SQS stores multiple copies of a message on multiple servers for redundancy reasons. On rare occasions, it may happen that one of the servers that maintain a copy of the message may not be available when receiving or deleting a message. If such a circumstance occurs, the copy of the message stored on the unavailable server will not be deleted, and it is possible that you may receive an additional copy when you receive the messages. For this reason, an application that is idempotent must be designed (that is, the application must not be affected if the same message is processed more than once).

Queue URLs: when creating a new queue, you must provide a name that is unique within the scope of all the queues owned by an AWS account. Amazon SQS assigns to each created queue an identifier called "queue URL" which includes the name of the queue and other components that Amazon SQS determines. Whenever you want to perform an action on a queue, you have to use the "queue URL".

Message-IDs: each message receives a "message ID" that Amazon SQS gives us back in response to a " SendMessage ". This identifier is useful for identifying the message, but to delete the message the receipt handle is needed, and it is not possible to do it with the message ID. The maximum length of a message ID is 100 characters.

Receipt Handles every time we receive a message from a queue; we receive a pointer for this message. The pointer is associated with the act of receiving the message and not with the message itself. To cancel the message or to change the visibility of the message, you must provide the receipt handle and not the message ID. This means that you must always receive the message before you can delete it (you cannot put a message in a queue and then recall it). The maximum length of the message pointer is 1024 characters.

Visibility time

When a component of our system receives and processes a message from a queue, the message remains inside the queue. Why isn't it automatically deleted? Speaking of a distributed system, there is no guarantee that the component will receive the message (a broken connection or a component blocked during the reception). For this, Amazon SQS does not delete the message, and it must be our application to delete it from the queue after receiving it.

Once received, the message still remains in its queue, but at the same time, you do not want the other components to receive the message again. Therefore the message is blocked using the " visibility timeout " which is a period of time during which Amazon SQS prevents others to receive the message.

There is a limit to the number of inflight messages that can remain in the queue, and this number is 120,000. " Inflight " messages are those messages that have been received but have not yet been deleted from the queue. If the maximum limit of 120,000 is reached, you will receive an OverLimit message error. To avoid this limit it is advisable to delete the messages once processed immediately, or it is also possible to increase the number of queues that process the messages.

Each queue is set with a default visibility timeout of 30 seconds; you can change this value for the whole queue. When receiving a message, you can also set a special visibility timeout value for received messages without changing the general queue timeout. If you have a system that produces messages that require a variable amount of time for processing and deleting it is recommended to create multiple queues with different visibility timeout values.

AMAZON EC2 ADVANCED WITH LOAD BALANCING AND AUTO SCALING.

These services are easy to understand when presented with practical examples. If you have an AWS account, the best thing would be to repeat all the steps you find in this article and personally check all the results on your management console.

Load Balancing

This service automatically distributes the traffic of our application between different EC2 instances. The interesting thing about the service is that the traffic will be divided only between the instances that are active and functioning, in fact, if some instance by chance had availability problems, the traffic to the latter would be disabled, and all connections would be diverted to the servers that have the ability to respond.

You can use the DNS error switching feature present in the Amazon Route 53 service to improve availability and create a second Load Balancer, as the Route 53 service will find the first load balancer in error, perhaps because there are no instances active correctly, traffic will turn on the second configuration. Below I am attaching an image in which an example scenario is represented.

Precisely for this reason, the service is not considered only as a balancing of traffic, but we can say that it also performs an availability function. Moreover, if we divide our instances into different areas, the load balancing service in the face of a general problem on the geographical area will only use the group of instances that will be in the functioning availability zone without loss of service.

Security: The Load Balancing service also performs a security function, in fact, it is possible to publish the Balancer on the internet but divert everything to a private network, in this way access from the outside is protected by the allowed ports and the EC2 instances remain in one network without internet access. In any case, the service can be configured in a VPC environment to create a completely private balancer.

Auto Scaling

This service allows you to automatically scale the resources present in Amazon EC2 both by increasing and decreasing them, based on predefined conditions. With this service, it is possible to increase the power required without interruption of service and to cope with any peak requests. To the same extent, it is possible to decrease it when it is no longer needed in order to keep general costs under control.

The service is suitable for applications that show sudden changes during the hours, days or weeks. Auto Scaling has no additional service costs, as it is included in the costs of using EC2. We can connect Amazon CloudWatch events to trigger scalability actions, which can take place within a group of instances in Load Balancer. (seen previously)

For example, we can define a condition that adds new EC2 instances with an increase of 3 instances at a time when the average CPU consumption exceeds 70% for a certain consecutive period of time. With the same technique, we can define a rule that eliminates instances when the average total consumption drops to

10%. There is no rule valid for all environments; you have to find the right compromise.

In the section dedicated to the Auto Scaling service, we can create different groups and link different scalability characteristics. Each group will take into account the actions taken and store them in a kind of log that can be consulted from the console. In any case, you can also activate the Amazon SNS service to receive notifications.

Load Balancing (configuration)

To try this feature, you need to go to our management console and create a Load Balancer. That we find in the main menu of EC2. During the creation phase, we will be asked for several parameters that we will analyze, and we will have to indicate the EC2 instances that we want to associate with Load Balancing. As you can see by not using other services, this association should always be done manually.

Before launching the creation of the Load Balancer, we check that we have a test environment to perform our tests, with at least one VPC, a public subnet and at least two active instances that we have some details that distinguish them. For example, in this tutorial, we have configured two web servers that show the same HTML page with one server indicating "SERVER A" and the other "SERVER B".

As we can see from this screen, the steps are simple, in the first step we have to indicate the name of the Balancer, the VPC we want to use and the ports on which we have to balance the traffic. In the second section, we will be asked for the parameters that allow the service to know when to consider an EC2 instance that is no longer valid and therefore suitable for not receiving more traffic.

Once the Health Check screen has been set, the one for defining the subnets that the Load Balancer must check should appear. In fact, as we have already mentioned, it is possible to balance the traffic on instances belonging to different areas of availability. In this tutorial for simplicity, I will choose only one.

We continue by indicating the EC2 instances that are part of this balance, now just indicate the ones that we have activated, but the service also allows you to remove or add new ones after creation. To perform a test I added only two instances in a single availability zone, and we will add these, they are two identical instances with ubuntu, but which will indicate a different string on the home page.

Once we have added these two instances, we move on to the tags screen, which for this tutorial, we can also ignore and confirm the screen. At this point, we should wait a few seconds and find ourselves the active Load Balancer. On the balancer menu, we can perform various operations and view all the information connected to it — both the operating parameters and some usage statistics.

In this screen, we find the first section (description) from where we can see the DNS name that we need to test the Load Balancer immediately. Instead in the following (Tabs), it is possible to view other information such as the assigned instances, the Health Checks, the monitoring statistics, the security groups, the listening ports and the management of the Tags.

Load Balancing (result)

To test the configuration, just open the browser and request the page indicated by the URL string of the Load Balancer 's DNS name. By making some consecutive HTTP requests, the response of the two servers that we entered in the configuration should appear on alternate pages. I am attaching below the result I have obtained.

If we want to perform more complex tests, just add instances to our Load Balancer and try the HTTP requests. I recommend, after all the tests, to terminate the instances used and delete the Load Balancer, so as not to generate costs.

Auto Scaling (configuration)

To configure this service, a menu is made available from the console, in which you find two main items: the first is called boot configuration and the other the Auto Scaling groups. In the configuration, you must specify the parts that must be assigned during the launch of an instance. So the AMI, the type of instance, the storage, the security groups, etc. In the group instead, the reference options for scalability must be inserted, therefore the minimum and a maximum number of instances, etc.

This screen represents the creation of a " launch configuration " which as you can see is very similar to starting an instance. In fact, they are an indication of the options that must be used when the Auto Scaling service starts new instances. Once the configuration is created, we can create a scalability group.

AMAZON CLOUDFRONT SERVICE FOR THE CONTENT DELIVERY NETWORK

Amazon Cloudfront service is a CDN (Content Delivery Network) system that allows the distribution of static content from different geographical locations to maintain low latency and therefore, better performance. In addition to exempting central servers from static requests, it also performs audio and video streaming functions without the need to install complex software on your web server.

If a user requests content present on Amazon Cloudfront, the latter will be directed to the nearest edge location and therefore with lower latency. If the content is present in the edge location, it will be immediately distributed. Otherwise, it will be recovered from the configured source, and a duplication request will be generated to serve the next requests made from that geographical point.

Introduction

When we request an HTML page, the process is not concluded immediately, in fact, the code of the loaded page is first analyzed, and then further requests are generated to load all the elements that make up the page itself, for example, images, stylesheets, javascript, fonts, etc., etc. So if in the requested page there are for example 30 different resources they will generate 30 single HTTP requests to the same server. Normally, but not always, the first request is dynamic processing, for example with PHP, ASP, Java, etc., while the others are static resources, and it is precisely on these that a CDN intervenes.

In fact, the task of a CDN and in this case that of Amazon Cloudfront is to divide and balance all the HTTP requests generated, leaving the dynamic ones to our web server and the static ones to the service itself. In this way, the greater workload and scalability problems related to static resources would all be delegated to the Cloudfront service. As you can easily guess, our web server would be freed from a very large number of HTTP requests.

Edge locations map

Terminology

Like all Amazon AWS services, before starting to configure the service, it is good to get familiar with the terms that are used. I list here below or the most important terms and then let's see a test configuration.

Objects: Objects are those files stored in our source that we want to be automatically distributed through the Cloudfront service. Objects include images, static files or anything that can be distributed via HTTP or Adobe RTMP the protocol used by Adobe Flash Media Server. Support for Microsoft Live Smooth Streaming has also recently been added. So we can store videos for use with Microsoft's proprietary player.

Origin Server: The origin server is the place where the original versions of the objects that we want to distribute with Cloudfront through the edge locations reside. The origin server can be an S3 Bucket or an HTTP server; the latter can be activated either on an EC2 instance or on a different server outside the AWS. If the objects are distributed via HTTP the origin server can be an S3 Bucket or an HTTP server; if they are streamed via RTMP, the origin must be an S3 Bucket.

Distributions: Once the objects are stored on the origin server, you must specify where they reside through a distribution that can be of two types:

Web Distribution - Distribution via the HTTP and HTTPS protocols. You can distribute images, CSS files, javascript, fonts, documents, etc ...

Streaming Distribution - Distributes digital content through Adobe Flash Media Server and the RTMP protocol. We can store video files.

Edge Locations: It is a geographic site where Cloudfront deposits copies of objects stored in the sources that have been specified in the distribution. If the edge location does not have the requested object, Cloudfront takes it from the origin server and distributes it to the end-user, then keeping a copy in the cache in the Edge Location.

Expiration: For each request of the same object, Cloudfront will distribute the object contained in the Edge Location cache until the object has expired. After the object has expired on the next request, Cloudfront will forward a request to the origin to determine if a more updated version of the object is available. By default, the object expires after 24h which resides in the

Edge Location cache. The minimum expiry time of the object is 0 sec, and there is no maximum limit.

Eventual Consistency: When a Cloudfront deployment is created, modified or deleted, it takes time before changes are propagated to the complete system. The distribution information eventually becomes consistent, but an immediate request for information may not show the changes. It usually takes a few minutes to achieve data consistency, but a high load on the overall system may increase the time required.

Costs

Cloudfront or S3?

Both Cloudfront and S3 distribute content, is it always better to use Cloudfront to do it? Not necessarily, it depends on our particular needs and on the geography of our users. Amazon S3 has been designed to store the original versions of the files and to guarantee high data durability. Cloudfront was designed to distribute content with very low latency; it was not designed for durable data storage. If you expect a high number of requests for objects, Cloudfront can provide higher performance than Amazon S3 alone. On a high number of Cloudfront requests, it is cheaper than S3.

Configuration

Amazon Cloudfront setup via console and online demo

Distribution creation

First of all, we must make sure we have a single place of origin available containing the objects that will have to be served by Cloudfront, then an HTTP server or an S3 bucket, with an exception with regard to the videos that must be served in streaming, the which must necessarily be stored on Amazon S3.

In our example we will use a scenario where the source server will be an S3 bucket that will contain two folders, one called images / and the other videos /, we will create two distributions, the first for static images/files and the other for streaming video RTMP of videos /.

Then, from the main menu of the service choose the " create distribution " option, you will be asked if you want to create a Web or RTMP type distribution, we will use both types of distribution in this example, for the moment we select the Web type one which will be dedicated to images and subsequently we will create one of the RTMP types.

Web distribution creation

Once we have selected the first type of distribution we will be asked for a series of parameters, I report below the most important ones to use in this first phase, then on the subsequent articles dedicated to Cloudfront, we will also see more specific options that are used for particular configurations.

Origin Domain Name: specify the origin of the objects that will be served by the CloudFront; in our case, indicate the S3 bucket that you have created for this purpose.

Viewer Protocol Policy: through this option, we can choose the access allowed to our resources in HTTP, HTTPS or both. It is also possible to request an HTTPS redirect if an HTTP URL address is specified.

Object Caching: choose whether to add a standard Cache-Control in the HTTP protocol or indicate a custom value called Minimum TTL.

Price Class: through this option, it is possible to control the general costs by choosing on which geographic regions it is possible to distribute. For example, we can choose, "only US and Europe", "only US, Europe and Asia" or all locations.

Alternate Domain Names: this option is specified when we want to map one of our sub-domains to the CloudFront one, so do not use the classic URL form abcdef.cloudfront.net of the service but a URL of the static.dominio.com type.

Logging: indicate whether to enable logging regarding access to this resource, we can specify a destination S3 bucket and a suffix to be applied to the file name, which can be the beginning of the file or the indication of a folder.

Distribution State: we can indicate whether, after the creation of the distribution, it is immediately active or is put in a "deactivation" state which will be activated manually later. With this option, we can also deactivate a distribution without cancelling its configuration.

Creation of RTMP distribution

As for the creation of this distribution, the parameters that will be required are much less, and in any case, they are the same as we have seen for the standard distribution, so see the list of previous options and also create an RTMP type distribution that we will use in the examples.

List of distributions

Once the distribution creation requests are finished, a list similar to this screen should appear where the status column should be indicated as "in progress" and only after a few minutes it should change to "deployed". Sometimes you just have to wait 5 minutes and sometimes 20, so arm yourself with patience.

Once the distributions have been released and are in an active state, we can begin to store our objects on S3 and recall them in an HTML page using the domain name that you find indicated in the distribution both in the general list and in the " distribution " section — setting".

AMAZON (SES) SIMPLE EMAIL
SERVICE CLOUD MAIL

Amazon SES is an email service (outbound-only) that allows you to send an email simply and economically. The service can be used for sending marketing emails (e.g. offers), transactional emails (such as order confirmations), newsletters, etc., etc. You only pay for the shipments you use, so you can send large or small quantities of email messages according to your needs without the need to subscribe to advance subscriptions.

Introduction

The sending of an email to the internet takes place through an outgoing mail server that takes charge of it and forwards it to the final destination. These mail servers can be the server of our Internet Service Provider (ISP), a company server or a mail server configured ad hoc. When using the Amazon SES service, the outgoing mail server becomes Amazon SES itself, although it is possible to continue to use your own mail server and then forward the emails to SES.

With Amazon SES you eliminate the complexity of implementing and maintaining an email sending solution within your company, in fact even if sending emails may seem a very simple function, in reality, it hides many complexities that we will try to see in the continuation of this article. By using the SES service, we can solve these aspects easily and without complex infrastructures.

What to check

If we had to take care of the problems concerning the sending of emails we would have to keep a lot of things under control, for example memorizing the% of emails that arrive at their destination and those that are blocked because they are considered spam, we should be careful not to send too many emails in the round of a short time because the ISP could judge the high number of mailings as an attempt to send SPAM and thus block the IP address of our server. Another aspect of managing would be to keep track of emails that are rejected (bounced emails) due to a shipping error or because the recipient's email address does not exist. In any case, we should not send back to these addresses or differentiate the new attempts.

Amazon SES can send notification messages when these problems occur and provide real-time access to statistics regarding the number of emails that have been sent and those that have not been sent for the reasons listed above. It will automatically manage the shipping times between the various emails based on our credibility and the history of past shipments, so as not to incur penalties.

Shipping tools

The most used and immediate method to send emails via Amazon SES is to use the Simple Mail Transfer Protocol (SMTP) which can be managed by all the email servers in circulation, with SMTP we can also use some programming languages such as for example the Java libraries.

Amazon console: this is the fastest way to set up the service and send some test emails, but once in production, you have to use the other tools. We can also use the console to read the statistics linked to our profile.

Amazon API: through this tool, you can implement direct calls to Amazon SES in your programs and send email messages related to specific events, for example, the confirmation of the order, happy birthday messages to your customers, etc. etc. The APIs that concern Amazon's services can be used with different programming languages according to the SDK package used.

Email Deliverability

If we want recipients to be able to read our emails and not be considered SPAM, we need to increase email deliverability, the percentage of emails that arrive at their destination. In order to maximize this aspect and know what happens in our shipments, the following steps must be carried out:

Understanding delivery problems: in most cases, emails always arrive at their destination, but in some cases, sending may not be successful. In these cases, you need to understand why and make different decisions based on different reasons.

Prevention: one of the biggest internet problems related to email is unwanted email or SPAM. The current ISP (Internet Service Provider) take several countermeasures to try to stem this phenomenon, so we must try to follow some specific rules in order not to fall into this category.

Stay informed: when a sending fails, or a recipient complains of the email they received (feature available on many ISPs), Amazon SES tracks these problems by sending notifications and keeping detailed statistics.

Improve the programs: once you understand all the reasons for sending failed and the problems associated with them you can also intervene to change the logic of our shipping program and improve it, everything will also depend on the technique used.

Terminology

Before using the Amazon SES service, you need to know some terms used by the service and the general concepts associated with them. In fact, even if the service is simple from the configuration point of view, in order to be used to its best, you need to know the mechanisms and controls that are hidden behind the service itself.

Bounce: When the delivery of an email fails and does not reach its destination, the recipient sends the message back to the origin server on Amazon SES. The reasons why the email may have been rejected are mainly two:

Hard Bounce: when there is a permanent error in sending the email, such as when the destination mailbox does not exist or no longer exists.

Soft Bounce: when there is a temporary error in sending the email, as could be the mailbox full or the ISP server unreachable.

Complaint (complaint): many email programs provide the ability to classify emails as SPAM and to send the notification to the service provider. In addition, many ISPs have a mailbox (e.g. abuse@example.net) where it is possible to forward the emails that we no longer want to receive. Both cases will turn out as if the recipient is asking the ISP to block unwanted emails. In these cases, the provider will send feedback to SES who will pass this information on to your account.

Suppression list is a list of addresses that Amazon SES does not consider valid (blacklist) because they have generated a hard bounce in the last 14 days. If you try to send an email to an address in the list, the call to SES is successful, but Amazon will treat this email as a hard bounce and will not send anything.

Verification: unfortunately, a spammer can falsify the header of an email by believing that it has been sent from another address. To maintain this relationship of trust with ISPs, Amazon SES requires that the person who sends is truly the person he claims to be. So consequently, the Amazon SES service requires that all the email addresses used for sending be verified. This verification can be done through the console or through the Amazon API.

Authentication: identifying is another way to be able to tell our ISP who we really are. When authenticating an email, you must provide clear evidence of the account owner and that the email has not been changed on the way. Some ISPs reject emails that are not authenticated. Amazon SES provides two different authentication methods: Sender Policy Framework and DomainKeys Identified Mail.

Sending limits: if an ISP detects sudden or unexpected peaks in the volume of emails or in the frequency of sending, it could label emails as spam and block them. For this reason, each SES account has a series of limits that regulate the number of emails that can be sent and the frequency with which they can be sent.

Content filtering: many ISPs use the content filter to determine if the emails that arrive are spam. The content filter analyzes the email in search of content that is sharable, and that can be considered spam, at which point the email is blocked. SES also uses " content filter " tools for emails that pass through the service.

Reputation: Amazon SES maintains a strong reputation with ISPs, and this is why it requires those who use their service to have a high-quality reputation level. The reputation level affects the email sending limits that Amazon SES imposes. If the emails are of quality, the limits are raised, if the emails are considered spam or the Bounce) the limits are lowered.

Use of APIs

It is possible to make calls to the SendEmail and SendRawEmail APIs, the amount of information that must be provided depends on which API is called.

The SendEmail API requires sender, recipient, subject, content and reply-to. When invoking this API, Amazon assembles a formatted email (MIME).

The SendRawEmail API allows us to format and send a raw message created by us, specifying: Headers, MIME and the type of content. This API is used for advanced email use.

Management console

If we select the Amazon SES service from the home page of our management console, we will immediately see the main menu on the side sidebar and some graphs with the most important information related to our account.

The Amazon SES main menu allows initial configuration operations such as SMTP setting, suppression list and sender verification both as a single email address and as an entire domain.

AMAZON CLOUDTRAIL
TO MONITOR AWS APIS

All the operations that are carried out on Amazon Web Services take place through API calls, which can be used by AWS internal processes, manual procedures via management console or application programs. Almost all services have logs available for specific operations, but it has always been difficult enough to keep track of everything that happened in our cloud computing environment. This aspect is solved through CloudTrail, and it is now possible to monitor everything that happens in our AWS account.

How does it work

Amazon CloudTrail captures API calls made by or on behalf of an AWS account and sends log files to an S3 bucket specified by us. It is possible to specify the destination bucket of the logs using CloudTrial within the management console or through the AWS CLI or the CloudTrail APIs. Basically, log files are encrypted using Amazon S3 (SSE) server-side encryption.

You can store all the log files in an S3 bucket for the period you want, but you can also define a lifecycle rule to archive them in Amazon Glacier or automatically delete them. Generally, CloudTrail sends a file within 15 minutes of the API call and publishes the new logs several times over time, normally about every 5 minutes. These log files contain all the API calls made by the supported services, and you can also publish a notification via Amazon SNS.

Use of the service

There are no additional costs for using CloudTrail, but the standard Amazon S3 rates are paid for the space occupied by the logs and for the possible use of Amazon SNS. Here are some steps to follow to use the service:

- Use the console, AWS CLI or the CloudTrail API to create a trail, which consists of the information that CloudTrail uses to send log files to S3.
- (Optional) It is possible to create a topic in Amazon SNS to which the service subscribes to send a notification when a new log file arrives on S3.
- Amazon S3 APIs can be used to retrieve logs.

- It is possible to use APIs, AWS CLI, or the console to update the trail.
- (Optional) AWS IAM (Identity and Access Management) can be used to control which AWS users can create, configure or delete trails, start and stop logging, and control access to the bucket that contains the logs.
- (Optional) It is possible to analyze the files generated by CloudTrail with one of the integrated solutions proposed by the partners, which give different functionalities, for example, detection of changes, troubleshooting and security analysis.

Configuration

To start the service, we can enter our management console, select the geographical region and the menu that relates to the CloudTrail service. If we have never activated the service, we will be presented with indications to create the trail:

In this screen, we have to indicate an S3 bucket, which can be created or selected from a list of existing buckets present in the profile. If we use the second method, we have to set the permissions for the bucket manually, if instead, we have it created from the management console this operation will be automatic.

Below we can indicate a prefix to be used in the log files, the inclusion of global services and the possible configuration of notifications via Amazon SNS.

Geographical regions

The service is tied to the region, which means that a separate trail is created for each region. By default, Trails contain information for events that occur in those regions, as well as global service events that do not belong to a specific region, such as IAM or AWS STS.

For example, if you have configured two trails in two different regions when you create a new user under IAM, the user creation event is added to the log information of both regions. If you configure the service to collect logs from multiple regions in a single bucket, IAM service events will be duplicated.

To prevent duplication, global events can be selectively included. One solution could be to enable the recording of global events in a single trail and disable it on all the other trails configured in the other regions that write in the same bucket on Amazon S3.

Log structure

There is a great deal of information stored in the CloudTrail logs, for example, it is possible to identify which users made the calls, the source IP address from which they were made and when the call was made. Unfortunately, however, all this information is not available in a readable format but must be processed by some program that extrapolates the data from a JSON structure.

```json
{
  "eventVersion": "1.01",
  "userIdentity": {
    "type": "Root",
    "principalId": "161858713267",
    "arn": "arn: aws: iam :: 161858713267: root",
    "accountId": "161858713267",
    "accessKeyId": "ASIAIXQ4G57LNG257VNQ",
    "sessionContext": {
      "attributes": {
        "mfaAuthenticated": "false",
        "creationDate": "2014-05-28T10: 13: 49Z"
      }
    }
  },
```

```
"eventTime": "2014-05-28T10: 55: 19Z",
"eventSource": "ec2.amazonaws.com",
"eventName": "TerminateInstances",
"awsRegion": "eu-west-1",
"sourceIPAddress": "88.114.16.93",
"requestParameters": {
 "instancesSet": {
  "items": [{
   "instanceId": "i-7204e733"
  }]
 }
},
"responseElements": {
 "instancesSet": {
  "items": [{
   "instanceId": "i-7204e733",
   "currentState": {
    "code": 32,
    "name": "shutting-down"
   },
   "previousState": {
    "code": 16,
    "name": "running"
   }
  }]
 }
```

        },

        "requestID":   "7a2b8969-94f4-474c-9714-
        482a1b2ca4a0",

        "eventID":   "fed7028d-0e42-4ebb-9e17-
        997e96ffb620"

        },

This example shows a log record in JSON format that refers to a simple stop request for an EC2 instance.

AMAZON SNS (SIMPLE NOTIFICATION SERVICE) FOR NOTIFICATION MANAGEMENT

Amazon SNS is a service that coordinates and manages the delivery or sending of messages between services, applications and mobile devices. Its use as we will see later is elastic and can be adapted to any application need that is needed. Many services that we find on Amazon Web Services are already prepared to send notifications through this service, which can also be implemented in our programs through the use of simple APIs and SDKs made available by Amazon.

Introduction

This service coordinates and manages the delivery or sending of messages to endpoints, also called clients. There are two types of clients: Publishers who communicate asynchronously to subscribers by sending a message through a logical access point called a topic. The subscriber (web servers, email addresses or SQS queues) receive messages or notifications through one of the supported protocols (SQS, HTTP / S, email, SMS) once they are associated with a topic.

When using Amazon SNS (as owner), you can create a topic and control access with policies that determine which publishers and subscribers can communicate with the topic. A publisher can send messages to a topic he has created himself, or to a topic for which he has been granted publication permissions. So also topics outside of your account.

Instead of having a specific destination address for each message sent, a publisher sends his message to a topic. Amazon SNS combines the topic with a list of subscribers who have subscribed to it and sends a message to each of them. Each topic has a unique name that identifies the endpoint; this name is used by the publisher to post the messages and by the subscriber to record the notifications.

Fanout scenario

There is talk of a " fanout " scenario when in Amazon SNS a message is sent to a topic, and this is replicated and sent to multiple Amazon SQS queues, HTTP endpoints or email addresses. This allows us to take advantage of a parallel asynchronous processing system. To clarify the concept, I attach the following image:

For example, let's consider an e-commerce application, this can be developed to send an SNS message to a topic every time an order is made for a product, the Amazon SQS queues subscribed to the topic will receive an identical notification for every new order. An instance connected to one of these queues could manage order processing, while another EC2 instance could be connected to a data warehouse for order analysis.

The " fanout " scenario could also be used to replicate the data sent in production to the development environment, in fact, it is possible to test the application by continuing to feed the test environment with data coming from production.

Let's take a test

As we saw previously, to do a complete test, we need to have a topic, a publisher and a subscriber. First, we need to create the topic as it is the communication channel between the other two components. Then we enter our management console, select the SNS service and choose "create topic".

To receive messages in a topic, you must register the endpoint and then create a subscriber; this can be a server, an email address or an SQS queue. Always from the service menu we select " My Subscriptions " and the action for the creation of a new element, we choose the protocol, the endpoint and we confirm the creation.

As a publisher, we can use the management console to test directly, which provides simple tools to send messages to the topic we have just created. Then select the publish button, specify the subject and description, send the message to the topic and check the message received.

Messages and protocols

If there are several subscribers who have registered for the topic, and they have different communication protocols, it is possible to send a different message to the topic according to the protocol. For example, we can send a short message for sending an SMS and a longer one for sending an email. The supported protocols are HTTP, HTTPS, EMAIL, SMS, JSON, SQS etc. Each of these protocols can have a message with different contents while maintaining the same sending.

Mobile Push Notification

With Amazon SNS, you can send notification messages directly to an app installed on a mobile device. Notification messages sent to a mobile endpoint can appear in the app as an alarm message, audible warning or badge updates.

The push notification services supported by Amazon:

- Apple Push Notification Service (APNS)
- Apple Push Notification Service Sandbox (APNS_SANDBOX)
- Amazon Device Messaging (ADM)
- Google Cloud Messaging for Android (GCM)

Notification services such as APNS and GCM maintain the connection to the apps and mobile devices associated with them. When apps and devices are registered for the service, they return a device token. Amazon SNS uses the token device to create the mobile endpoint and to send it the notification messages.

Amazon Storage Gateway for corporate and cloud connection

Amazon Storage Gateway is a service that directly connects your IT environment with a storage infrastructure present in Amazon Web Services through a software appliance to be installed within your company. This allows secure storage of your data in the AWS cloud system resulting in scalable and convenient storage. Amazon Storage Gateway offers two different types of storage, one based on volumes and the other based on tapes.

Storage Models

The service as we have already seen offers two storage models, one based on volumes and the other on tapes, the possible configurations are different and in this article we will try to analyze the most important ones:

Volume Gateway - provides storage volumes that can be mounted as simple iSCSI devices and configured without major problems on the servers within your company. The way to configure volumes:

- Gateway-cached volumes

- Gateway-stored volumes
- Gateway-virtual tape library (VTL) - provides a virtual tape infrastructure for backing up data in Amazon S3 or long-term archiving in Amazon Glacier which allows a considerable reduction in costs for this type of operation.

Cached volumes

In this case, the data is stored in the Amazon S3 service (simple storage service) and only a copy of the data with more frequent access is kept in the local storage. Operation is exactly like a cache system . gateway cached volumes substantially offers effective savings on the total costs of primary storage and minimizes the need to scale storage within your company, maintaining low latency of access to the most used data.

At this moment in the cached gateway, the volumes can go from a minimum of 1GB to a maximum of 32TB and must be rounded to GigaByte. Each gateway that is configured as a cached volume gateway can support a maximum of 20 volumes for a maximum capacity of 150TB. When application server data is sent to volumes in AWS, the gateway initially stores this data on local disks called cache storage before uploading it to Amazon S3. Cache storage acts as permanent storage for data that is waiting to be loaded into the Amazon S3 environment.

Stored volumes

When low latency is required for the entire data set, the gateway can be configured so that all data is stored locally and asynchronously backed up to S3 via a series of snapshots. This type of configuration provides a reliable and inexpensive offsite backup that can be restored locally. If you also need to replace your infrastructure in the event of disaster recovery, you can start EC2 instances.

The data written by the stored volume gateway is stored on local disks within the company, while asynchronously a backup is made in Amazon S3 in the form of an EBS snapshot. The size of the volumes ranges from a minimum of 1GB to a maximum of 1TB. Each gateway configured as a stored volume gateway supports up to 12 volumes, for a maximum capacity of 12 TB. To prepare the data on Amazon S3, the gateway stores the data inside the upload buffer. The gateway uploads the data in the upload buffer through an SSL connection to the AWS Storage Gateway service active in the AWS cloud. Then the service stores the encrypted data in Amazon S3.

Virtual tape library

With this function, it is possible to archive all the backup files in Amazon Glacier and therefore take advantage of an inexpensive backup system and long-term data archiving. The system is compatible with most existing backup software both in Linux and windows and provides a virtual tape system that scales smoothly according to the needs of your company, completely eliminating the problem of managing, maintaining and scaling a complex infrastructure of physical tapes.

The virtual tape is comparable to a physical cartridge even if the data resides in the cloud environment. Like physical cassettes, virtual tapes can also be empty or contain data; virtual tapes can be created using the console or using APIs. Each gateway can hold up to 1500 tapes or up to 150TB of data at a time. The size of the virtual tape is configurable and can be between 100GB and 2.5TB.

A " Media Charger " VTL is similar to a physical loader that moves tapes within the library, in slots or tape drives. Each VTL is supplied with a charger that is directly usable by applications via the iSCSI standard.

Hosting option

In the previous paragraphs, we have seen that the virtual appliance is always positioned in the company data centre, in reality, it is possible to position this virtual image also in the cloud environment on EC2, which is very useful in case of disaster recovery. In fact, if your data centre goes offline and there are no hosts available, you can activate a gateway on EC2 that continues the alignment operation. Amazon Storage Gateway also provides a prepackaged AMI image that contains the gateway.

AMAZON ELASTIC TRANSCODER
VIDEO TRANSCODING SERVICE

The video conversion can be considered relatively simple when it comes to converting some video for personal use or use one of the many software transcoding available on various platforms. But when the need for conversion must be resolved in the server environment with the processing of many conversions and with large videos then the problems begin, in fact not only the technical aspect becomes complicated but also the necessary power becomes important and unmanageable from a dedicated server let alone a hosting service.

Amazon Elastic Transcoder

It is from this need that the Amazon Elastic Transcoder service was born, which allows the conversion of multimedia files stored within Amazon S3 into various formats and which can be viewed by different playback devices. For example, it is possible to convert large-high-quality digital media files into formats that users can play on mobile devices, tablets, web browsers and TVs.

To use this service and manage a high-quality video conversion in a fast and scalable way, we don't need to install any software on our server, let alone study the hundreds of parameters that regulate a video transcoding. As mentioned previously, we only have to store the original video on the S3 storage and start processing with Elastic Transcoder, which will think about giving us the finished result.

General scheme of the service

Components

The video conversion service provided by Amazon is divided into four main components; let's see together the general features:

(1) Jobs: perform the transcoding job. Each job can convert one file up to 30 different formats. For example, if you want to convert a media file into 6 different formats, you can create a single job that performs this conversion in the six required formats. When creating a job (job), you must specify the name of the file you

want to transcode and the name that Elastic Transcoder will use in the result files.

(2) Pipelines: are the queues that manage the transcoding jobs. When creating a job, you need to specify which pipeline you want to assign to the job. The service will begin processing jobs within a pipeline in the order in which they were added. If you configure a transcoding process in more than one format, Elastic Transcoder creates the files for each format in the order in which the formats were specified in the job.

A fairly common configuration is to create two pipelines: one for processing normal priority jobs and the other for high priority processing. Most jobs would end up in the normal queue, while the high priority queue would only be used when immediate transcoding is required.

A pipeline can process more than one job simultaneously, and the time required to finish a job varies significantly based on the size of the file you want to convert and the specifications assigned to the job. As a result, jobs will not necessarily be completed in the same order in which they were created. Jobs can be temporarily interrupted by pausing the pipeline.

(3) Presets: these are templates (called templates) that contain most of the settings for transcoding multimedia files from one format to another. Elastic Transcoder includes some predefined settings for the most common formats, for example, various versions of iPhone or android. The preset you want to use must be specified when defining and starting a job.

(4) Notifications: Elastic Transcoder and Simple Notification Service (SNS) can optionally be configured to follow a process: for example when a job starts, when it ends, when warning or error conditions are detected, etc., etc. SNS notifications can be configured when creating a pipeline.

General scheme of the components

Log into

Elastic Transcoder is a RESTful web service that uses HTTPS and JavaScript Object Notation (JSON) as the message format. The code of our application can request directly to the API of Elastic Transcoder. When using the REST API directly, you need to write the code needed to sign and authenticate requests. Elastic Transcoder also provides a graphical console for interactive management. The console can be used to perform all the operations that can be performed using the Elastic Transcoder API.

Converting a video

Now let's see together the steps necessary to perform our first video conversion: Connection through our account on AWS, create an S3 bucket or two if you want to differentiate the input files from the output ones, create a pipeline, create a preset or use them a standard provided by the Elastic Transcoder service, create a new job and monitor its completion, check the output files.

Creating a pipeline

Let's assume that we have an AWS account and we know how to create an S3 bucket, so let's see how to create a pipeline for use with Elastic Transcoder. We go to our management console and select the service from the usual list, you can find it in the Application Services group. The first thing you will be asked for is the creation of a pipeline where you will need to specify the following parameters:

1) In the first part, we have to insert a name of the pipeline; normally we use a prefix name to which to add

the queue type, for example, normal or high priority, I often use the format transcoder.domain.standard or final .high.

2) Name of the S3 bucket where the original videos will be stored. You can also use this as a destination, but in this case use different folders, for example, you can create folder inputs, outputs and covers (for covers).

3) Indicate the Authorization role, in the beginning, you can use the standard one, but when you go into production, create an IAM user suitable for the specific purpose. Default permissions can also be specified in the S3 bucket definitions.

4) Indicate the name of the S3 bucket where the converted files will be stored, and the name of the one in which the covers will be stored, as already mentioned you can use the same bucket indicated as the source and manage the division by folders.

5) As the last parameter, indicate the SNS notification system and the information you want to activate, progressing, warning, completion or error. Obviously, you must first create and configure an SNS topic suitable for the purpose.

Creating a Job

Now that we have our job queue, we can define a JOB for requesting a video conversion. We always go to the management console and select the JOBs item in the service section where we find the "create a new job" button. Once selected, we should enter different parameters as follows:

1) The first major thing we need to know is the name of the pipeline in which our work must be submitted, for example, the standard one or a high priority one to immediately perform the conversion without waiting for the conclusion of the standard ones.

2) Indicate the name of the source file to be converted and the prefix to be used in the output files, normally on this last option a folder is indicated. In any case, this prefix is added to the file name indicated as output.

3) Indicate the conversion preset, which contains all the technical parameters related to the quality and general characteristics of the video. Amazon provides many pre-configured presets, in any case for special needs, to be able to create new ones.

4) Know the name of the output file, the starting point and its duration, the creation of a cover, the rotation

value and some technical parameters such as the frame rate, aspect ratio, interlaced and container. Many of these options can be "auto".

AMAZON (IAM) IDENTITY AND ACCESS MANAGEMENT

he Amazon Web Services service called IAM (Identity and Access Management) allows you to manage security regarding the control and use of resources and services made available by Amazon. Using IAM, it is possible to manage groups, users, roles and permissions to grant or deny the use of services linked to an account.

With this service we can avoid using the credentials of our main account and create a certain number of users and specific authorizations for services or groups of services, this will allow us to protect the root user and make the granting and revocation of authorizations a much safer function.

Introduction

Without this service, organizations with multiple users would have to create multiple accounts, each with their own billing and subscription to Amazon services, and employees should also share their credentials on a single AWS account.

Without IAM, you have no control over user and systems activities and what they can do and what AWS resources they could use.

Amazon IAM solves this problem by allowing organizations to create multiple users (each user can be a person, a system or an app) who can use the services, each with its credentials and all controlled by a single AWS account.

AWS identity and access management is a feature linked to an AWS account and is made available at no additional cost. Obviously, the costs of the AWS services used through their IAM users will be charged. The advantage of this is that you can manage billing and subsequent payment in a single account.

Functionality

Most of the features made available by Amazon IAM are manageable through the management console that you can see in the previous screen. The first actions that are normally performed are the creation of groups, users and roles, as you can see from the screen all these operations are performed globally, and therefore it is not necessary to select any geographical region.

The groups are used to assign permissions to a set of users to manage, without having to specify security rules for each individual user. The users can be created with its own access rules and then be placed in groups. As regards the roles, it is possible to define specific entities that we can assign, for example, to EC2 servers or applications.

Other features that we can manage from the console are MFA activation to log in with double authentication and timed password. Change password policies with custom organization level policies. Get a URL address that we should use to log in to our IAM users. In fact, the login on Amazon can only be used for the root account while the new URL for IAM users. On the example screen, you will find this field referred to as the IAM Sign-in URL.

Migration

If your organization already uses Amazon Web Services, migrating to Amazon IAM can be easy or very demanding, it all depends on how AWS resources are currently allocated. Here are the three possible scenarios:

A single AWS account: in this case IAM migration is quite simple because all AWS resources are already managed under a single AWS account, so just stop using the root account and configure a new IAM administrator user.

Multiple AWS accounts and each represents a division: if the divisions do not need to share resources or users, then migration is simple. Each division can maintain its own account and use IAM separately from the other divisions. You can also use billing consolidation, which would allow your organization to receive a single invoice for all AWS accounts.

Multiple AWS accounts and each one does not represent a division: if AWS accounts have to share resources and have users in common, migrating to IAM will be very difficult, in fact in this case you need to move the resources you want to share under a single account and since there is no automatic system to transfer resources from one account to another, you must recreate all the resources under the new AWS account.

Terminology

As is now our habit when we present an AWS service for the first time, we always list the most used terms in such a way as to have less difficulty in reading the official documentation. As for Amazon IAM, the most important terms that you need to know are the following:

Accounts: If you already use AWS, you will already have become familiar with AWS accounts and their features. With IAM, an AWS account remains basically the same, except that an account can now manage users under it. An account is the first entity that is created when you start using the services and is the owner of all the resources created under it and pays for all the activities that the resources generate.

Role: is an entity with a set of permissions that another entity assumes to make calls to access AWS resources. The person taking on the role uses temporary security credentials to make calls.

Resources: a resource is an entity of an AWS service with which a user can interact, such as an S3 Bucket, an SQS queue, and so on.

Permissions are the concept of allowing or denying an entity, such as a user, group or role, some kind of access to a resource. For example, Mario is given read permission on an S3 bucket called example_bucket.

Policy: it is a particular document that provides a formal declaration of one or more authorizations. With Amazon IAM, you can assign a policy to an entity, and its permissions are declared in the policy. Multiple policies can be assigned to an entity.

If you want to assign the same policy to multiple users, we recommend that you put users in a group and assign the policy directly to the group.

The ten best tips

1. Secure your AWS account credentials.
2. Create individual IAM users.
3. Use groups to assign permissions to users.
4. Grant minimal privileges.
5. Configure a password policy.
6. Enable MFA for privileged users.
7. Use roles for applications on EC2.
8. Delegate using roles instead of credentials.
9. Periodically rotate your credentials.

10. Use conditions to increase safety.

Permit simulation

Through the management console, we can simulate the permissions and users that we have defined in our IAM environment without having to test the real environment and use account resources. To test it, just go to Policy Simulation, enter the user, the service, the action and press the key called " Run ". Directly on the console, you will get all the results and details of the access test.

As you can see from the previous screen, you can try many actions and different users by launching a single simulation and analyze the results in detail for every single simulated action. The selection of the service and actions are guided with pop-up selection menus that appear when you select the entry fields.

10 TOP BEST PRACTICES (IAM) IDENTITY ACCESS MANAGEMENT

1. Secure your AWS account credentials

Any request to Amazon Web Services requires access credentials, which are used to check that you have the right permissions to access resources. The access keys are also used to make requests programmatically, especially for API calls.

In any case, it is advisable never to use the credentials of the main account, which in addition to giving full access, also allows access to billing data, credit cards and personal data. We recommend that you always follow these steps to secure our main account:

Use a strong password to protect your account.

Enable AWS multi-factor authentication (MFA) for your AWS account.

Do not create any access keys related to the main account unless strictly necessary and delete any access keys created.

Never share passwords or access keys of the main account with other people, as unlike IAM, it is difficult to revoke permissions.

2. Create individual IAM users

Create individual IAM users for anyone who needs access to your account. Create a user with administrative privileges for yourself and use this user for all management tasks. Well, manage the permissions that are assigned to each individual IAM user and in case of need, revoke them or create new credentials.

As you can see on this screen, users can be managed from the console where it is also possible to manage access keys, assign passwords, define permissions, add users to groups, delete users, assign MFA, etc., etc.

3. Use groups to assign permissions to users

Instead of defining the access permissions for each individual IAM user, it is preferable to create groups related to the various work functions (e.g. administrators, developers, administrators etc.) and define the relevant permissions for each group and then assign the IAM users to the groups. This makes it easier to manage permissions, making changes only on the single group and not on all users. If a user within the company changes his duties, it is possible to move the person under the corresponding group without resetting his authorizations.

As for users, we can also manage groups from the console; we can define permissions, add users, define new groups or delete others. Although the use of groups is recommended when you have many users, I personally always use it, even with few users, I still find it simpler and more orderly.

4. Grant the least privileges

When creating policies in the IAM environment, it is good to follow the standard security recommendations by granting the minimum privilege, that is, granting only the permissions necessary to perform the required task. Determine what users need to do and then create tailored policies that allow users to perform only the necessary operations. It is safer to start with a minimal set of permissions and only grant additional ones if necessary, rather than starting with the permissions that are too lenient and then trying to restrict them later.

A good way to start is to use the predefined models; these include the authorizations for the common use cases (administrator, power user, etc.) of the single services.

You can also create your own criteria to set permissions more precisely. To do this, you need to be familiar with the syntax with which policies are written, and how policies are evaluated when there is more than one policy in effect during a resource request.

5. Configure a password policy

If users are given the opportunity to change their password, they need to make sure that it is created with some complexity. In the Password policy section of the IAM console, you can set options for passwords, minimum length, upper case, lower case etc. I recommend generating a user password only in case you need to give access to the console, in other cases only use the access keys.

The customization that concerns the password policies can be set at the general account level, and therefore, all existing users will be affected. If you have many users to manage, I suggest you allow the password to be changed.

6. Enable MFA for privileged users

For greater security, multi-factor authentication (MFA) can be enabled for those users within IAM who have administrative privileges or who access AWS resources considered critical for the company.

Through this feature, access to your account will not only include a user and password pair, but a request will be added for a timed password that can be generated by a physical device that you can buy by following the links that are indicated to you or via a smartphone application like Google Authenticator.

If you use a smartphone application, the configuration is very simple, just ask for MFA activation from the console and place your camera on the code generated by Amazon which will automatically configure the new account. Once configured correctly, enter the time code twice as shown.

7. Use roles for applications on EC2

Applications running on EC2 instances need credentials to use AWS services and to provide them securely, IAM roles must be used. The role is an entity that has a set of permissions but is not a user or group. Moreover, the role does not have a set of permanent credentials as a user can possess them, the credentials are associated with whoever assumes the identity, or if an EC2 instance is used, IAM dynamically provides temporary credentials.

When you start an EC2 instance, you can associate an IAM role with the instance as a boot parameter. Applications running on the EC2 instance can use role credentials to access AWS resources. The permissions assigned to the role determine what applications are allowed to do.

8. Delegate using roles instead of credentials

You may need to allow users of another account to access AWS resources. In this case, it is better not to share the access keys or credentials between AWS accounts, but it is recommended to use IAM roles. You can define a role that specifies which permissions are granted to the IAM user of another account and from which AWS account IAM users are allowed to take on the role.

9. Periodically rotate your credentials

Change passwords and access keys periodically and make sure that all IAM users in your account do the same thing. To make it easier to rotate your credentials, activate the option to let users manage passwords. All the operations concerning the modification of the credentials or the creation of new access keys can be found in the user's screen in the "security credentials" section.

From this screen, you can also change the console access password for IAM users and optionally also activate two-pass authentication. If you use AWS service access keys for many IAM users, remember to revoke old keys from time to time and create new ones.

10. Use conditions to increase safety

Define the conditions under which the policies intervene and enable access. For example, it is possible to write conditions that specify a range of enabled IP addresses, or it is possible to specify that a request is authorized only in a specific period of time. It is also possible to define conditions that require the use of MFA or SSL. In this case, you can request that a user authenticates with MFA in order to grant him permission to terminate an EC2 instance.

As you can see from the screen there is no wizard at the moment to enter the conditions on the permissions, so we have to enter them manually according to the syntax that you find in the official documentation of the conditions.

AMAZON RDS MANAGES A RELATIONAL DATABASE IN CLOUD COMPUTING

Amazon Relational Database Service (Amazon RDS) is a web service that simplifies the implementation, management and scalability of a relational database within cloud computing that affects Amazon Web Services. Many web applications use a database that resides in the same machine as the application, this for a non-scalable environment and that requires modest power can be fine, but if conditions change, an external database must be used which, as we will see, makes the more scalable and simpler environment from a systemic point of view.

Some advantages

This service takes on many aspects related to the management and maintenance of relational databases, operations that can sometimes be difficult. From a systemic point of view, all the configuration part is simplified, and all the complexity concerning the installation of the database software is cancelled, which can have different characteristics if used in different operating systems. Through Amazon RDS, we are all ready to use, and we do not have to worry about anything. The following advantages are listed in the official documentation:

When buying a server, you need to consider the amount of CPU, memory, storage and IOPS. With Amazon RDS, everything related to the part of the database can be managed separately, and resources can be scaled completely independently. For example, if you need CPU, IOPS or more disk space, it is sufficient to allocate the resources you need only in the RDS service.

Amazon RDS manages rescues, software patches, automatic malfunction detection and recovery. All operations performed in a private environment require complex configurations and installation of additional software.

Through this service, it is possible to have automatic backups that are performed according to your needs; it is also possible to create snapshots that allow a very fast and reliable restore operation.

High availability can be achieved by using a primary and a synchronous secondary instance, which can only be run when certain problems occur. Read-only replicas may also be used for performances.

You can use different SQL databases and choose the ones you are most familiar with: MySQL, PostgreSQL, Oracle and Microsoft SQL Server.

In addition to the security of the database package, you can control who can access RDS databases using AWS IAM to define users and permissions. You can also protect our databases by putting them in a virtual private cloud.

One of the few disadvantages of an external database is its latency, in fact, unlike a local database, network transmission must be added to the response time, but in reality, this apparent disadvantage in a complex environment turns into a great advantage that it also significantly improves performance.

DB instances (database)

The basic structure of Amazon RDS is called a DB instance which consists of an isolated database environment in the cloud. A database instance can contain multiple user-created databases and can be accessed using the same tools and applications that are used with a stand-alone database instance. You can create and / or modify a database instance through a command line (Amazon CLI), using the Amazon RDS own APIs or the classic interface on the AWS Management console.

Each DB instance manages a different database engine, MySQL, PostgreSQL, Oracle and Microsoft SQL Server are currently supported. Each database engine supports its own characteristics, and each version can include specific details. In addition, each database engine has a set of parameters called (DB parameters group) which control the behaviour of the database to be managed.

The storage and computing capacity of an instance is determined by its instance class. You can select the class that best meets your needs; if they change over time, you can modify the instances without intervening in the configuration of your applications. Obviously, the available classes have different prices which you can consult in the Amazon RDS cost section.

For each DB instance, it is possible to select from 5 GB to 3 TB of associated capacity. Each instance class has a minimum and maximum storage requirements for the

DB instances that are created. It is important to have enough storage so that the databases have room to grow and that the engine functions have room for content and logs. Instance storage is available in two types: standard and IOPS. Standard storage is allocated on Amazon EBS volumes and connected to the DB instance, while IOPS uses optimized volumes and a configuration stack that provides additional capacity.

You can run a DB instance in a virtual private cloud using Amazon's Virtual Private Cloud (VPC) service. When using a virtual private cloud, you have control over your virtual network environment: you can select your IP address range, create subnets and configure routing and access control lists. The basic features of Amazon RDS are the same both in a VPC environment and not. There is no additional cost to run the instance in a VPC environment.

Geographical regions

Like all Amazon AWS services, it is possible to choose the geographical region on which our services must be active; therefore also for Amazon RDS and the DB instances that we should start, it will be possible to choose the regions and zones of availability. On this topic, we have dedicated a specific article called "AWS Infrastructure" which I recommend you read for any further information.

In any case, it is possible to say that each geographical region is divided into several zones which are called: availability zones. Each zone has been designed to work independently and independently, even if other areas suffer a failure. Availability zones within a single region communicate with each other with a low latency network to allow for advanced availability solutions.

Multiple database instances can be run in different availability zones using the Multi-AZ call option. When using this option, Amazon RDS creates and maintains a synchronous standby replica of a database instance in a different availability zone. The primary database instance is replicated synchronously through the availability zones linked to the selected region in order to provide data redundancy, failover support, eliminate I / O blocks and minimize latency peaks during database backup operations.

Security Group

A security group controls access to database instances by allowing access to specific IP address ranges or specific EC2 instances. Amazon RDS uses three types of security groups: DB, VPC and EC2. In other words, the former controls access to DB instances that are not in a VPC; the latter controls access to DB instances that are within a VPC and the third controls access to an EC2 instance.

DB Parameter Groups

It is possible to manage the configuration of a DB engine using the DB Parameter Group which contains the configuration parameters of a database engine that can be applied to one or more instances of the same type. If you don't specify a parameter group at the same time as creating a DB instance, Amazon RDS will apply a default DB Parameter Group. The default group contains the default settings for the selected database engine and the " instance classes " associated with DB instances.

In this screen, I report the parameters related to a MySQL instance, and as you can see it is how to manage my.cfg file in standard configuration, the only difference is that not all parameters are editable, in fact, they are blocked to make our database work on a virtual instance that will run in the AWS environment.

Cost calculation

Costs are billed according to the following criteria:

Instance class: the cost is based on the class of the instance that will be used (e.g. micro, small, large, xlarge) on standard, memory-optimized and micro/small instances.

Running time: costs are charged per instance hour, which is equivalent to a single instance running for one hour. For example, both a single instance running for two hours and two instances running for an hour consume two instance hours.

Storage size: the disk space allocated to the database instance is billed per GB per month. If you increase the disk space in the month, the invoice will be proportionate.

I / O requests per month: the total number of I / O storage requests made in a billing cycle. The same calculation is done in the Amazon EBS environment.

Backup storage is the storage space that is associated with database backups and with every active snapshot that is taken. Increasing the retention period of backups or performing multiple additional database snapshots increases the required storage space. Amazon RDS provides backup storage of up to 100% of the space allocated for database provisioning at no additional cost.

For example, if you have 10GB of storage allocated for the database, Amazon RDS will provide up to 10GB of backup storage per month at no additional cost. Most databases require less storage for backup than their primary data set, so if you don't keep multiple backups, you don't have to pay anything for the backup storage. Backup storage is free only for active DB instances.

Data transfer: the transfer of data in and out of your database instance. Read this documentation well on this cost, as a lot of traffic based on the configurations is free, for example, the transfer between Amazon RDS and an EC2 instance is not charged as a service fee.

In addition to the normal Amazon RDS rate card, it is possible to purchase reserved DB instances, which allow you to pay a one-off fee to book an instance for one or three years at much more advantageous rates. Same option as in Amazon EC2.

NoSQL database introduction and use in cloud computing

For some time now, we have been talking about NoSQL databases (not only SQL), which are indicated as an alternative to the classic RDBMS relational databases. In reality, as we will see, they are not a complete alternative to SQL databases, but they are a different thing that can be used for data structures in highly scalable environments. The most important factor that brought this technology to its current popularity is the fact that today the computational power supply is completely different than in the past, and we have gone from vertical to horizontal scalability.

Scalability concept

When we talk about vertical scalability we mean the increase in power within the same server, therefore we increase the processors, disks, RAM etc., etc. While horizontal scalability means when we add multiple servers for parallel processing of an application. Obviously, in the first solution, we have a limit which is dictated by the maximum power that a single computer can reach, while in the horizontal one in principle we can add servers to infinity :)

In any case, even if vertical scalability has an intrinsic limit, it is still the technology that has carried out our personal workstations and the majority of corporate servers so far, which in some cases even came to have a single server (mainframe) that managed thousands of users simultaneously.

This went well as long as the connections remained closed in a more or less large border represented by the organization's local network. With the advent of the internet, everything has changed, and the number of connections that an application could receive is not only much higher, but it is also completely unpredictable. In this new scenario, the SQL relational databases have begun to show large performance limits which have been partially solved by the databases called NoSQL.

Available solutions

Currently, there are several NoSQL database solutions. However, the weak point of these solutions is that they all use proprietary protocols compared to relational databases that over the years have reached excellent standards, which allow the passage from one database to another in a simple way. So at the moment before choosing a NoSQL solution, it is good to find the one suitable for your needs and run many tests before choosing, as a further change would be very laborious.

I list below some NoSQL databases, some run in a cloud environment such as Google and Amazon, while others are stand-alone and therefore can be downloaded and installed directly on the servers. Obviously, if our application runs in a cloud environment, it is preferable to use those already integrated into the service that manages scalability well and reduce the time and complexity of installation.

CouchDB: it is a document-oriented database where the document is the only subject of memorization, in this database, there are no tables, but the documents are saved directly in the database through a JSON structure, this solution is designed and indicated for the web applications with which it shares several common aspects.

MongoDB: it is a very performing document-oriented database that maintains some aspects similar to SQL databases; this aspect makes it very interesting for those who want to switch to this technology coming from the relational one. I recommend you read the official documentation as there are so many interesting functions.

Redis: this open-source database is of the key-value store type and offers a server-by-key data structure, which can contain strings, hashes, lists, sets and sorted sets. Redis is written in C language and is suitable for all Unix like systems even if there is a beta version for windows environments. The documentation in Italian is very scarce.

DynamoDB: it is a NoSQL database present in Amazon Web Services, it is defined as an ultra-scalable database that manages different availability zones and can be integrated with Elastic MapReduce and Amazon S3 for backup to online storage. Its main feature is linked to the simplicity of configuration in complex environments.

Cassandra: is a database developed by Facebook to solve some problems related to the high traffic of its social network. In 2008 Facebook released the open-source sources which are subsequently managed by the Apache Software Foundation. At this moment, this database is also used by Twitter and Digg.

Google Big Table is a database developed by Google and is based on compressed data, at the moment even if it is very performing it remains limited by the fact that it can only be used in the Google App Engine environment. Right now, it is used in many google products itself such as Google Maps, Gmail, Youtube, etc., etc.

The complete list of NoSQL databases is actually much longer, at the moment I have brought you the ones I thought were the most interesting, in any case, I suggest you go to this page => http://nosql-database.org/ where you will find a complete list.

General structure

We have seen that there are many solutions, all of which have different characteristics, but they have in common that they do not have a rigid structure as regards the data schema that we find in the relational databases. In fact, in a relational context we must first define the schema with the fields, the types of storage, the keys, etc., and only then can we perform the reading, modification and cancellation operations. In NoSQL, this process is not necessary, and the storage can have different structures.

The implementation methods are different based on the chosen NoSQL database; not all solutions start from the same principle. Let's see some features:

Column Family: the information is divided into rows and columns like the schemes, however, the number of columns is not predetermined and may vary between one row and another. There are two types of solutions; one called the standard column and the other super column.

Graph: these databases store information with graph structures, making access with object-oriented languages and applications more efficient. Some databases in this group are Neo4j, FlockDB, AllegroGraph and GraphDB.

Key / Value: in this case, the data is stored in an element that contains a key together with the values, this method is the simplest to implement, but also the most inefficient if the operations concern only a part of an element.

Document store: it is the evolution of the key/value method, compared to relational databases that store data in tables with fixed fields, these are put into a document that can contain a structure with different fields and different lengths.

Some disadvantages

Like all things, even in NoSQL databases, there are not only advantages, for example, if on the one hand, this technology solves the performance problem, on the other, it makes reading the data for a much more complex statistical analysis. It is no coincidence that I know of the structures which, by switching to MongoDB for web applications, then convert some information on a MySQL database to analyze it more easily.

Another major disadvantage is that the migration process to another database is much more complex than relational solutions. In my work, I have repeatedly witnessed several RDBMS migrations, for example, in the case of companies that were acquired and where it was necessary to convert the data on the database of the purchasing company. I have seen migrations from

DB / 2 to MySQL from MySQL to Oracle without major problems, but for example, a conversion from MongoDB to DynamoDB had some problems :)

AMAZON ECHO

The world of Alexa has undoubtedly been the protagonist of these days of discounts in Amazon sauce. It could only be like this: the Amazon Echo family comes directly from the house of Jeff Bezos, the promised cuts were very palatable, and some of the models have even sold out, but it will never come again.

But to better explode the value of Alexa, it is possible to combine an Amazon Echo with other devices that can make the home environment "smart." Such as? Here are some examples.

Alexa, turn on the light

The smart bulbs ("smart bulb") are the device that, with a small investment and big surprise, may return with more immediate voice interaction power. All you need is to issue the command "Alexa, turn on the light," and the bulb, properly configured through the app, react accordingly.

Two models by way of example:

- Suprema Astute, a dimmable LED bulb, warm white
- Smart 8W bulb, 800 Lumen, colored

How much is the amazed look of a child in front of the magic of the light that lights up alone? How much is a light turned off with the voice when you are already lying in bed or on the sofa? Cyber Monday offers a possible answer.

Video surveillance, baby monitors and security

Whether it is for video surveillance, to monitor a baby while sleeping, or to monitor the interiors of its home remotely: Alexa can open up a range of opportunities through the simple combination of shooting systems whose cost is a continuous downside and that for this Cyber Monday have become one of the most explored attractions.

Soundbar and beyond

Thanks to Alexa, a normal TV soundbar can turn into something more, bringing the music of Amazon Music or Spotify directly to the center of the living room and in high quality.

iRobot Roomba and the house is clean

Why not clean the floor of your home with just the effort of thinking and saying it? After all, it is sufficient to issue the appropriate command, and the robots of the iRobot Roomba series are ready to obey, acting in complete autonomy to eliminate all traces of dust, animal hair, and residues of any kind.

Three models are still discounted in these hours, with different ways of cleaning and analyzing the surrounding environment for an intelligent movement between the obstacles of the house:

- iRobot Roomba 671
- iRobot Roomba 960
- iRobot Roomba i7156

Echo Wall Clock with Alexa

A wall clock with the artificial intelligence of Alexa: it is Echo Wall Clock, one of the accessories for the home proposed by Amazon, between the protagonists of the Black Friday

Among the features a digital display with 60 LEDs that can be useful to show the timers set: for example, it is enough to say "Alexa, put a 12-minute timer" to see the countdown start and receive an alert when you reach the end. The diameter is 25 cm (dimensions 254x254x 41 mm, weight 380 grams), and the feeding is done with four AA batteries included in the package at the time of purchase.

Communication with Alexa devices takes place thanks to the integrated Bluetooth module. The watch, therefore, represents a nice accessory for those who already have an Amazon Echo in the kitchen, where the use of a timer is of fundamental utility and where the hands are often smeared: "Alexa, put the 10-minute timer for pasta".

Amazon Echo: what it is and how it works

Browsing on Amazon, you came across the page dedicated to the devices in the Echo range and, intrigued by their presentation; you immediately started looking for some more information about their operation. So you ended up here, on this tutorial of mine, hoping to find the answers to your doubts. Well, I'm glad to tell you that you've come to the right place at the right time! In the following lines, in fact, what are Amazon Echo and what they are able to do, illustrating in detail the potential of Alexa, the personal assistant that animates these devices.

To simplify the discussion as much as possible, we can say that the Amazon Echo are speakers of various sizes that, once connected to the power supply and the Internet, allow you to perform various operations using voice commands. To animate them, there is Alexa, a personal assistant who resides in the cloud and allows you to perform many operations: listen to music from streaming services, set reminders, and alarms, listen to the news, get weather and traffic information, buy products on Amazon and much even more.

Furthermore, the devices of the Echo range perfectly integrate with the main home automation systems and therefore allow the control of Smart devices at home with the voice. Another important feature is the integration with many third-party services and apps (the so-called skills) and the possibility of connecting them to speakers and various external devices via cable or Bluetooth. Interesting, isn't it? Then don't waste any more time: read on and discover all there is to know about Amazon Echo, their prices and their characteristics. Find all of the details below.

Amazon Echo devices

Before delving into the operation of Amazon Echo devices and discovering, in more detail, what they are able to do, it seems only right to list them all and illustrate their peculiarities.

It should be noted that the functions linked to Alexa are the same on all Echo models: what changes is the format of the device, the power of the audio (both output and input), integration with home automation systems, connections for external speakers and the presence of the display. To learn more, read on.

Amazon Echo Flex

Amazon Echo Flex is the cheapest device in the Echo family. It is a small speaker that connects directly to the power outlet (similar to what you do with some compact Wi-Fi repeaters) and offers a USB port to charge/power your devices or install a Smart night light (from buying separately). The ideal solution to enter the world of Alexa or to have the possibility to transport the Amazon assistant easily from one room to another in the house.

Amazon Echo Dot

Amazon Echo Dot is the "little one" of the Amazon Echo family. It consists of a "dot" (hence the name "Dot") of 43 x 99 x 99 mm for 300 grams of weight. Includes a single 41 mm loudspeaker, 4 long-range microphones, and a 3.5 mm audio output for connection to external speakers (a connection that can also be made wirelessly, via Bluetooth).

Also noteworthy is the presence of keys to adjust the volume and deactivate the microphone, plus a luminous ring, located on the top of the device, which indicates the status of the same and of the requests made by the user.

It is available in colors anthracite, light gray, it mottled gray and mauve. It can also be purchased bundled with an Amazon Smart Plug. It is also available in a variant with an integrated LED display (to display the time), which costs a little more.

Amazon Echo

Amazon Echo is the right device for those looking for a personal assistant and, at the same time, a good speaker for listening to music. It is, in fact, a cylindrical speaker with an elegant fabric covering that includes a

3 "(76.2 mm) neodymium woofer and a 0.8" (20 mm) tweeter, for powerful sound and enveloping. It measures 148 x 99 x 99 mm for 780 grams of weight and has 7 microphones to capture the user's voice even from long distances.

It has keys to adjust the volume and mute the microphone and a light ring (on the upper part) that indicates the status of the device and the requests made to Alexa. It also offers a 3.5mm audio output for connection to external speakers (a connection that can also be made wirelessly via Bluetooth). It is available in colors anthracite, light gray, it mottled gray and blue-gray.

Amazon Echo Plus

As its name suggests quite easily, Amazon Echo Plus is an enhanced version of Amazon Echo, heavily focused on listening to music and home automation. In fact, it has a cylindrical speaker of 148 x 99 x 99 mm for 780 grams of weight, with a 76 mm woofer inside, a 20 mm tweeter, 7 microphones, and a Zigbee hub thanks to which it is possible to control home automation devices based on the Zigbee system without relying on third-party applications.

It also has a 3.5mm output for connecting external speakers (which can also be connected wirelessly via Bluetooth) and, more importantly, an audio input that allows Echo Plus to be used as an audio output for other devices. Also noteworthy is the presence of the sensor to detect the ambient temperature and a support for wall mounting. The keys and the light ring are the same as those on the Amazon Echo base.

It is available in anthracite, light gray, and mélange gray colors and can also be purchased bundled with a Philips Hue White bulb. Undoubtedly the best Amazon Echo available at the moment and worth more than the base model (as long as you care about the quality of your music and you have a home automation system based on Zigbee technology).

Amazon Echo Studio

Amazon Echo Studio is the ideal solution for those looking for a device to be used to listen to high-quality audio. It includes as many as five speakers that offer powerful bass, dynamic mids and crisp highs with Dolby Atmos and Sony 360 Reality Audio technologies, for an all-round 360-degree sound. Going further into the technical, it includes a 13.3 cm and 330 W woofer, a 2.5

cm tweeter, and three 5 cm midranges, combined with a 24 bit DAC and a 100 kHz amplifier.

It includes a Zigbee hub for Smart device control and can be paired single or in pairs with Fire TV devices, to give an extremely immersive audio experience. It measures 206 x 175 mm for 3.5 kg of weight and is available only in dark color.

Amazon Echo Spot

Amazon Echo Spot differs from the devices of the Echo family mentioned above due to the presence of a display and a front camera. In fact, it presents itself as a sort of "eye" on whose front stands the "usual" luminous ring (which indicates the status of the device), a 64mm color touchscreen that always remains on to show useful information (now, weather, last engagements, etc.) and a frontal camera. Above, it has physical keys to adjust the volume and turn off the microphone, while on the back it has a 3.5mm audio output for connection to external speakers (a connection that can also be established wirelessly, via Bluetooth).

Despite the small dimensions (104 mm x 97 mm x 91 mm for 419 grams of weight), thanks to the built-in

36mm loudspeaker, it can reproduce a good sound (even if a little lacking in the bass). The 4 microphones, then, allow you to control it even from important distances. The presence of the screen allows you to view videos (eg, news on the news or the TV series of Amazon Prime Video), check the device manually (as well as by voice), view the footage of the surveillance cameras, make video calls and view information that otherwise you could only listen (eg, the steps necessary to cook a dish).

It is available in colors white and black and can be purchased bundled with Amazon Smart Plug, a set of light bulbs Philips Hue color, or a set of light bulbs Philips Hue White. It represents the right choice for those looking for a more versatile device than the other Echo and does not have any particular requirements in terms of audio quality.

Amazon Echo and Amazon Echo Plus can be paired together to create a pair of stereo speakers and/or can be paired with a subwoofer. To establish the connection, the speakers must be online and connected to the same network and, of course, must be placed in the same room.

Amazon Echo Show

Amazon Echo Show is the complete Echo device, which focuses heavily on the use of visual content, such as videos and information from the Internet. It is equipped with a 10.1 " HD touchscreen, a 5MP front camera, an audio compartment composed of two 2" drivers with a passive radiator for bass and a Zigbee hub, thanks to which it is possible to control the devices for home automation based on this system without using third-party applications.

It is available in black and white colors. It is sold individually, combined with a Philips Hue bulb, in a bundle that also includes a Philips Hue bulb and an Echo Spot or in a bundle with two Echo Shows and a pair of Philips Hue bulbs.

Amazon Echo Show 5

The Amazon Echo Show 5 is a reduced version of the Ecco Show, with a 5.5 " and 960 x 480-pixel color touch screen, 1MP camera, integrated camera cover, and button to turn off the microphone and camera. Its audio sector sees the presence of a 1.65 "and 4 W loudspeaker. It supports Wi-Fi and Bluetooth. It is sold alone or in bundles, including a Smart plug or video door phone (Ring).

Amazon Echo Input

Amazon Echo Input is not a speaker like the other Amazon Echo models, but a device that, associated with an external speaker, be it Bluetooth or only with a wired connection (using the classic 3.5mm jack), allows you to use voice commands of Alexa with the latter. It includes four microphones and is available in both white and black. It is also sold bundled with several well-known speakers, such as Ultimate Ears BOOM 3 and Megaboom 3. That said, it can be combined with any cash or Bluetooth cash. It should also be noted that it does not support calls and messages via Bluetooth.

What can you do with Alexa

Before evaluating the purchase of an Amazon Echo, you will almost certainly want to find out more in detail what Alexa can do, the personal assistant that animates the devices produced by the e-commerce giant.

Like any self-respecting personal assistant, Alexa is able to set reminders and alarms, provide weather information and steal information from the Internet to answer user questions (eg, "Alexa, why is the sky blue? ", "Alexa, what is Napoli doing? "," Alexa, what is the distance between the sun and the Earth? "and so on). It also lets you know the price and buy products on Amazon and to set up morning and evening routines, through which, for example, to listen to the most important news of the day, to receive information on the weather conditions and to discover the list of one's personal commitments.

A separate chapter, then, deserve the functions related to multimedia use: thanks to its integration with services such as TuneIn, Spotify and of course Amazon Music, Alexa manages to play songs, albums, playlists or radio stations requested by the user (eg, "Alexa, let me listen to jazz music ", "Alexa, let me listen to Michael Jackson's Smooth Criminal ", "Alexa, let me listen to Rai Radio 2" etc.). In addition, you can ask Alexa to read the books in your Kindle library, play your favorite podcasts, and more.

Among the strengths of Alexa, as already mentioned above, there is also home automation: if you have Smart devices compatible with Amazon Echo, you can ask Alexa to turn lights on and off, open the blinds, view the video surveillance cameras (in the case of Amazon Echo Spot) and so on.

There is also fun: Alexa, in fact, can tell jokes, suggest films for the evening, and, thanks to some skills created by third parties, even formulate riddles, play quizzes, and play Chinese morra.

What are the skills? Simply one of Alexa's most interesting features, which allows Amazon's personal assistant to expand its capabilities to virtual infinity. To simplify the concept as much as possible, we can think of Alexa's skills as "apps" that are installed in your account (therefore, they are automatically activated on all the Amazon Echos in your possession) and allow access to services, sites, and applications. Third parties through precise voice command.

For example, it is possible to install the aforementioned games or service skills such as JustEat (to repeat orders previously made or to know the status of your current order), SuperGuidaTV (to learn about the TV programs of the evening), Rai Giornale Radio (for listen to the latest news from the GR Rai) and the list could go on forever.

If you are wondering, the Amazon Echo devices listen to what the user says only when they are activated via the "Alexa" command (or one of the alternative commands that you can set using the Alexa app). They do not "spy" continuously what is said at home. Furthermore, by connecting to this Web page and logging into your Amazon account (or by going to Settings> Alexa Account> Alexa App History), you can view and manage the history of all the voice commands given to your Echo.

If you want to learn more about Alexa and its potential, visit the Amazon Echo purchase page and click on the button Discover what Alexa can do, which is located on the left or, alternatively, visit the Amazon page with frequently asked questions related to Alexa and Amazon Echo devices.

HOW TO SET UP AND USE YOUR AMAZON ECHO SHOW

Amazon's powerful and manageable Alexa can now be seen and heard. The personal assistant, only once, has taken a step forward with Amazon Echo Show Seeing is believing: the Amazon Echo Show review Looking at the truth: Amazon Echo Show Review Does a voice assistant speaker really need a touchscreen? The $ 230 Amazon Echo Show certainly represents a compelling case, with flash video briefing capabilities, song lyrics, and on-demand streaming of supported security cameras.

The headlining feature of the device, currently available only for Amazon Prime members, is Amazon Prime. Is Amazon Prime a good deal? Amazon Prime seems like a big deal, but is it so? Let's find out the benefits to see if they are worth $ 99 a year. Read more in the United States, it's a 7-inch touchscreen that shows everything you can imagine, including Amazon video content, music lyrics, flash video briefings, and weather forecasts.

Echo Show - Black Echo Show - Black Buy now on Amazon $ 229, 99

While the touchscreen is a new feature, Echo Show offers all the other fantastic features of any Echo device, including the sound of filling the room, eight microphones, and the possibility of being heard from a crowded room.

If you have an Echo show, this guide is for you. We will deal with everything you wanted to know about Echo Show, including what the device is, how to configure the connected device, how to control a smart home, specify what skills are, solve common problems, and much more.

Here's what to expect:

1. Unboxing and setting up your Amazon Echo Show
Family profiles

2. Teach at Amazon Echo Show New Skills
How to find and enable skills | Skill categories

3. Control your Smart Home with Amazon Echo Show
Adding and removing a Smart Home device | Connection with cameras | Group creation and Scene discovery

4. Additional features on Amazon Echo Show

Video call | Explanation of drop-in | Voice messages | Watching videos | Shopping on Amazon

5. Troubleshooting the Amazon Echo Show
"Alexa" command which does not activate Amazon Echo Show | Amazon Echo Show cannot connect to the Internet | "Alexa" on Amazon Echo Show responds accidentally or randomly | Other Echo devices in your home respond at the same time

1. Unboxing and setting up your Amazon Echo Show

After opening an Amazon Echo Show box, you'll find the following items included:

- Amazon Echo Show (white or black version)
- A power cord and an adapter
- An introductory brochure
- A small guide with some basic Alexa commands

The most important thing to do before connecting Echo Show is to download the Amazon Echo app for your iOS or Android device. While technically you can use Echo Show without the app, it's a great way to interact with the device and customize different settings.

Once the Eco Show is connected, you will need to select a language, enter Wi-Fi credentials, and enter information on your Amazon account using the touchscreen. Since Echo Show can only be purchased from a Prime member, an account is required to use the device.

Thanks to two 2-inch stereo speakers that provide the best sound profile of any echo so far, an important first step is to head to the app and connect all the applicable music services. Open the Amazon Alexa app and go to the side menu. You will then need to select music, videos, and books.

You can choose from several different music options to play on Echo Show - including music from Amazon, Amazon Music, Spotify, Pandora, iHeartRadio, TuneIn, and SiriusXM streaming services.

Some choices, like Amazon Music and TuneIn, do not require a subscription or any login information. But you have to be a subscriber to use SiriusXM and Spotify.

As a fun touch, especially for closed karaoke singers, many Amazon Music songs will automatically display lyrics and covers on the screen. To activate or deactivate those, just say "Alexa, activate/deactivate the texts."

At the top of the Echo Show, you will see three different buttons. On the left is a Do Do Not Disturb button that turns off both the camera and the microphone. The other two are volume control buttons to control the speakers without an Alexa command.

It is also possible to connect Eco Show to another speaker for audio output via Bluetooth. To do this, just say "Alexa, go to Settings" or find the settings option by scrolling down on the screen. Choose Bluetooth. After making sure that the Bluetooth speaker you want to use is in pairing mode, it will appear in the list of available devices. Select it on the screen and then follow the instructions.

Family profiles

If more than one person in your home wants to manage their music library and other features, Echo Show can support multiple users called home profiles.

The person you wish to add must be present. In the app, go to the menu sidebar and select Settings> Accounts> Family Profiles. You will then need to follow the instructions on the screen.

Once added, the other person can view your Prime Photos on Echo Show. You also authorize them to use credit cards associated with your Amazon account to make purchases. They can also access traffic and personalized news, their music content, the shopping list, and the to-do list. For a complete overview of these features, see our Amazon Echo custom profile article Customize your Amazon Echo for multiple user profiles Customize your Amazon Echo for multiple user profiles Has your Amazon Echo become a family favorite? Do all purchases go to your credit card? Here's how to assign each member of your family their profile on a single Echo device. Read more.

When multiple accounts are set up, you can simply say, "Alexa, what account is this?" And "Alexa, change account" if necessary.

If you never need to remove another account, go to Settings> Accounts> In an Amazon home with [name]. Select Remove next to the specific user you are trying to remove Hit Leave if you want to remove yourself. You will have to press Remove again to confirm.

Certainly note that once another account is removed, it cannot be added to any other household for six months.

2. Teach your Amazon Echo Show new skills

Once you have created your Echo Show, the most important thing you need to know is skills. Skills feed the Echo Show and all other Alexa-enabled devices. The best way to think about skills is that each is an app controllable by voice.

Currently, there are more than 15,000 different skills to choose from. They range from ordering a Domino pizza to playing scary noises and much, much more. While some skills are not so smart 20 Echo Skills That Show Alexa's Not Always So Smart 20 Echo Skills That Show Alexa's Not Always So Smart Despite all the things you can do with Alexa out of the box, its extensibility through Skills is much more intriguing.

Some Echo Show abilities make use of the touchscreen, but most are still designed primarily for other audio-only Echo devices. That being said, the number of abilities that use the Echo Show screen continues to grow.

Unfortunately, at the moment, there is no way of knowing if a specific skill is optimized for the device screen. Hopefully, it will change as the number of skills increases.

How to find and enable skills

There are several ways to search and enable skills for your Echo Show. Besides being able to control all the options available on the Amazon Skills Portal, probably the simplest and most convenient path is the use of the companion app.

From the side menu bar, select Skills. You can view a number of different curated lists showing the new and recommended trending abilities. A search bar is at the top of the page if you know exactly what you are looking for. To browse all available skills, tap the Categories next to the search bar.

On each skill page, you can see some specific voice commands, a description of skills, customer reviews, and the option to receive support regarding the skill.

When you find an interesting skill, press the Enable button. Some options require access to an accompanying service while most are ready to use.

And if you know the name of the specific skill, it's even easier. Just say, "Alexa, activate [name of the skill]."

Skill categories

Here are all the skill categories you can select from:

- New arrivals
- business Finance
- Connected Car
- Education and consultation
- Food beverage
- Games, curiosities and accessories
- Health and fitness
- Lifestyle
- Local
- Movies and TV
- Music and audio
- news
- News and humor
- Productivity
- Shopping
- Smart home
- Social
- Sports
- Travel and transport
- Utility
- Weather

3. Control your Smart Home with Amazon Echo Show

While the Echo Show can perform a huge number of different tasks, something it currently excels in is controlling a smart home. The ecosystem of Alexa compatible devices is huge and is getting bigger almost every day.

The best way to find out if a smart home device is compatible with an Echo Show is to look at Amazon's Echo Smart Home page here.

Adding and removing a Smart Home device

If your device is compatible with Echo Show, make sure you also download the manufacturer's companion app.

Next, open the Alexa app and select Smart Home from the side menu. Choose Devices and then open the Alexa Smart Home Store.

You can browse or search for the ability of the corresponding device. Then select Enable. This could trigger a process to connect your device to the service.

Finally, Alexa will have to discover all the devices. This can be done through the app menu by selecting Smart Home> Devices> Discover. You can even say, "Alexa, discover the devices." You can see all the devices available in the app or let Alexa tell you how many devices were found.

There are two major exceptions to this discovery process. If you own Belkin WeMo devices or Philips Hue lights with the original circle-shaped version 1 bridge, you will not need to enable a skill. They should be found automatically when devices are detected. With the Hue bridge, be sure to press the top button before starting the discovery process.

If at any time you need to remove a smart home device from the Echo Show, go to the Smart Home section of the side menu. After selecting Devices, you will need to press Forgotten on each device to be removed. Just to note, it is also important to delete the device from the manufacturer's companion app.

Once the device is connected, simple voice commands can be used to control the processes. The complete list of commands can be found here.

Connection with cameras

A great exclusive for Echo Show is the ability to connect several smart cameras like configuring security cameras and avoiding common mistakes How to set up security cameras and avoid common mistakes In this article, I'm going to explain five of the most common mistakes that people make when installing their security cameras. I hope it helps you avoid making the same mistakes. Read more. Currently, cameras from famous manufacturers such as Ring, Arlo, Nest, August, EZViz, Vivint, Amcrest, Logitech, and IC Realtime are compatible.

You can add a compatible camera just like any other smart home device using the method above.

Remember to remember the name of your camera. So just say "Alexa, show [camera name]" and the screen will show a live video feed with audio. When you have finished watching the camera feed, you can say "Alexa, stop", "Alexa, hide [camera name]" or even "Alexa, go home".

Group creation and Scene discovery

If you install more than a few smart home devices, it's a good idea to create some groups. This makes it much easier to control your home with a voice command. Instead of having to tell Alexa to adjust each device individually, you can, for example, create a group called "Bedroom". Just saying "Alexa, turn off the bedroom lights" and everything will be done quickly and easily.

To create a group, go to the Smart Home section from the side menu. After selecting Groups, select Create group. You can then customize a name. It is better to use names with 2-3 syllables and avoid those that start with the same first word. You can then specify which devices to add to the group.

Another way to customize the installation of a smart home with the Echo Show is through the Scenes. Instead of creating scenes, you'll scan other smart home devices already available for all applicable scenes already created. The feature will provide Alexa with voice control of existing scenes from devices such as Philips Hue and Logitech Harmony Elite bulbs.

Although it is not possible to create your own scenes, they provide a great way for easier control of existing devices. To find the available scenes, go to Smart Home> Scenes from the side menu.

4. Additional features on Amazon Echo Show

There's no need to worry; the Echo Show does more than just check smart home devices. Here is a rundown of some other fantastic features you can explore.

Video call

Thanks to the touchscreen, the microphone, and the 5-megapixel camera, an extraordinary feature is a possibility of using the device for video calls to anyone with an Echo Show or Alexa app. Just like the other Echo products, it can also complete voice calls and voice messages. How to use the Voice Calling and Amazon Echo Messaging in 3 easy steps How to use the Amazon Echo Voice Calling and Messaging feature in 3 easy steps The Amazon Echo device and Alexa have been busy learning some new tricks. Long requested by users, messaging and voice calls add another level of utility to the widespread voice-activated speaker. Read more.

Video calling is very similar to other services like Apple's FaceTime, but the completely hands-free operation is unique.

You will need to access the Alexa app to configure and customize the function. Select the Conversations part of the app, which is the central option in the black bar at the bottom of the app. It looks like a comic book.

After confirming your name and surname, you will need to verify a phone number via an SMS message. When this happens, anyone with your phone number in their contacts will be able to use the Alexa app or the Echo device also to call or send messages to the user.

But you can block individual contacts if necessary. To do this, select the Contacts icon in the Conversations section of the app. Scroll down to the end, then press Block contacts.

When you are ready to make a call, it can be done to anyone with the Alexa app, any other Echo device, and even a regular phone number. Just say "Alexa, call ..." followed by the name of whom you would like to contact. You can even say each digit of a phone number.

You will hear a ring. If no one answers, Alexa will tell you that the contact is not available. When you're done with a call, just say "Alexa, hang up".

To make a call from the Alexa app, select the Contacts icon in the Conversations tab, then select the person you want to call. The layout is similar to what you find when making a call on your smartphone.

As a classy touch, the mobile number you have linked to your Amazon account will be displayed on the recipient's caller ID when making the call as a normal phone number.

When you receive a call, the Echo light strip turns green, and Alexa announces who is calling. There are two possible options for telling Alexa: "Alexa, Answer" or "Alexa, Ignore."

The smartphone will also display a notification that a call is coming in and from whom it comes.

Explanation of the drop-in

While the Drop-In function is available on the entire Echo line, it is particularly useful on the Echo Show. Anyone with the Alexa app or another Echo Show can hear and see anything within range of the device when it performs a Drop-In.

AMAZON PRIME VIDEO

Have you ever heard of Amazon Prime? Well, this special service is offered by Amazon to those who have decided to make a Prime subscription, receiving numerous benefits! One of these is Amazon Prime Video, which will allow you to watch movies and TV series on demand.

In fact, all Amazon Prime subscribers have a package of films and TV series to watch in streaming, as well as the exclusive Amazon Studios series.

HOW AMAZON PRIME VIDEO WORKS

Amazon Prime Video is the free service for subscribers to Prime that allows you to watch hundreds of exclusive movies and TV series in streaming.

The main Amazon Prime Video features offered to its subscribers:

Visible everywhere: You can use Amazon Prime Video on any device you want, where and when you want, via browser or the Amazon Prime Video App for smartphones and tablets, even offline once videos are downloaded.

X-Ray: You can use the X-Ray function that will allow you to get information about actors, songs, curiosities and much more, on a section of films and TV series.

Save data traffic: Manage data consumption independently, while downloading or watching videos, choosing the resolution and other features that will allow you to balance the consumption of the smartphone Giga.

HOW TO SEE AMAZON PRIME VIDEO

As mentioned above, you can see Amazon Prime Video wherever you want. To view Prime Video from your PC, just visit the Internet page dedicated to the Prime Video service and browse the gallery of films and TV series present, if you are already a subscriber.

To see Prime video from mobile, instead, you can download the dedicated App for Android and iOS, log in with your Amazon account subscribed to Prime, and you're done.

If you plan to see Amazon Prime Video on TV from the comfort of your living room sofa, you need to know that you can do it using one of the following devices:

Smart TV: If you have a smart TV you can download the Prime Video application (compatible with many models) ;

SmartBox: If you do not have a smart TV, you can buy a SmartBox that will make your smart TV practically a lower cost, and you can, therefore, enjoy numerous apps to use on your TV (including Prime Video). Find out more about the Android TV box in our dedicated article;

Home consoles: You can also download the Prime Video App on consoles like Playstation and Xbox and watch streaming movies;

Smart Fire TV Stick: This is a device manufactured and sold by Amazon itself. The price is around 60 euros (though it is often sold with 20-30% discounts), and you can see Prime Video and all the streaming services you are subscribed to, simply by inserting it into your TV's HDMI port.

How many Amazon Prime Video devices do you support simultaneously?

So far, we have listed all devices that support Amazon Prime Video, but how many devices can you use Prime Video at the same time? This factor is the Achilles' heel of the service, since, unlike its biggest rival, Netflix, Prime Video can support up to three devices simultaneously. In any case, not a small figure, considering the subscription price!

One last thing! Amazon Prime Video costs 0 euros, or rather, it has no additional costs to the Prime subscription and, therefore, for just 3.99 euros a month or 36 euros a year, you can take advantage of all the services offered by the Prime subscription.

Guidebook: This is how you see Amazon Prime on TV

As an Amazon member, you can receive Prime Video on many different devices like smartphones, tablets, PCs, or laptops. Of course, Amazon Prime comes naturally on the big TV to advantage. How you can watch the streaming service on the TV, you can find out here.

Install the Amazon Prime app on the Smart TV

Many smart TVs have the official Prime Video app preinstalled. Simply press the home button on your TV and then go to the app store. (Of course, the TV must be connected via Wi-Fi or LAN cable to the Internet).

After the app is installed on the TV, it will be displayed in the quick access (launcher). Now you have to log in once with your Amazon customer data. Some devices ask you to enter a registration code to associate Prime Video with your Amazon account. The on-screen instructions will guide you through the process.

The official Prime Video app is available for Sony *, Samsung *, Panasonic *, LG *, Hisensc *, and Philips * TVs. But not every smart TV supports all functions such as subtitles or live streaming.

You do not own a smart TV, or your TV is not supported by any official Amazon Prime app? Then there are other ways to watch Amazon Prime Video on TV:

1. Transfer Amazon Prime from the computer to the TV

Launch the browser on your laptop or PC, log in to Amazon Prime Video *, and then transfer the screen to your TV with an HDMI cable.

2. Mirror the Prime App on the TV

Many TVs have the standard Miracast / Screen Share, which allows a connection between mobile devices and TV. If this feature is present, enable Share on the smartphone or tablet to pair both devices. Now you see on TV exactly what can be seen on the mobile device display. If you start a video in the Prime App, it will now run on the big screen.

3. Stream Amazon Prime through Chromecast

If your TV does not have a miracast function, then you can help out with the Chromecast * (about 40 euros). The small stick from Google will plug into the HDMI input of the TV, where it will act as a receiver for your iOS or Android mobile device. In our guide, we'll explain step by step how to watch Amazon Prime Video on Chromecast.

4. Prime video via Fire TV stick to the TV

Amazon itself offers the Fire TV Stick, which is available in the standard version * (40 euros) and in the deluxe version * (60 euros) with 4K quality. While the Chromecast is just a receiver for the TV, the Fire TV Sticks are stand-alone minicomputers that you can use directly and extend their functions with apps as you like. Prime Video is already preinstalled here.

5. Stream Amazon Prime on the game console

The popular consoles have an official Prime Video app, with which you can see all the content on the TV. Supports: Xbox, Xbox One (Model S and X), PlayStation 3, and PlayStation 4 (Standard, Slim, and Pro) as well as Nintendo Wii U. Unfortunately, the Switch has no Amazon Prime app.

If Amazon Prime Video does not work: Solve typical problems

The video has been charging for ages, the picture and sound are out of sync, or the purchase is always aborting ... Amazon Prime Video sometimes has the quirks that it shows in the form of error codes. We'll show you how to solve them.

For the movie night, everything is ready, the light is set perfectly, the drinks are cooled - but the film just will not start. Instead, Amazon Prime casts video with four-digit error codes that will not help you. What to do? We help you!

Here are all the issues that Amazon Prime Video can give you - and we'll give you the answers. That a movie or a series does not load, can be one of the problems. A failure to buy videos, a lack of security on your browser, or an asynchronous soundtrack can be annoying as well. Do not panic! Find the solution here.

1. Problems in Prime Video and related error codes: Here are the solutions

Error playing videos (possible error codes: 1007, 1022, 1060, 7003, 7005, 7031, 7135, 7202, 7203, 7204, 7206, 7207, 7230, 7235, 7250, 7251, 7301, 7303, 7305, 7306, 8020, 9003 or 9074.)

Error in Google Chrome with playback due to the Widevine CDM (possible error code: 7017)

Video and sound are out of sync

Problems with the security log in Windows (possible error code: 1002)

Problems with ordering or payment (possible error codes: 2016, 2021, 2023, 2026, 2027, 2028, 2029, 2040, 2041, 2043, 2044, 2047, 2048, 2063 and 7035.)

The PIN does not work anymore (possible error codes: 5014 or 5016)

2. Error playing videos

One of the most common mistakes is related to playing, playing the videos. Typical error codes may be: 1007, 1022, 1060, 7003, 7005, 7031, 7135, 7202, 7203, 7204, 7206, 7207, 7230, 7235, 7250, 7251, 7301, 7303, 7305, 7306, 8020, 9003 or 9074 ,

Such difficulties occur in connection failures or inadequate equipment requirements. The wrong setting in the user account is possible. The following solutions can solve your problem:

No matter whether you use Prime Video in the browser, on the TV, or the smartphone app: Log in to Amazon again. Problems related to the user account can be fixed as often.

" New boat is doing well! "The classic is often the best solution: restart the device. Turn off your computer, smartphone, or router (last: unplug!), Wait about 30 seconds, and then restart the device. Try Prime Video again.

Is your Internet just overloaded? Pause all other Internet activity while using Prime.

Your Prime Video app, browser, or computer, or smartphone may be out of date. Update all applications and operating systems. It's also helpful to have a look at Amazon's information on device requirements.

Check the internet connection. It can also be a problem with your Internet service provider. The network connection may even be problematic only with streaming services.

Turn off VPN or proxy services if you use them.

4. Video and sound are out of sync

As long as the video is running, everything is fine. Because of: If the soundtrack of the film a bit too early or too late, that can make the evening of the movie extremely dull. So you also get this problem solved:

Change the picture quality. Just click on the gear icon above and change the video quality, ideally one level worse. Then click on the 10 second back button several times.

Previous problem resolution does not work in the mobile Prime Video app. Instead, you can change the language here by tapping the balloon icon at the top. Then tap the 10 second back button several times. Then switch back to the desired language.

Does the problem continue? Then delete the browser cache. You can do this in the settings of your browser. Mobile app users stop and restart the app.

5. Problems with the security protocol in Windows

Error 1002 is often related to the security log. In Windows, this may not be transmitted or is simply not up to date.

TLS 1.2 or 1.1 may not be enabled in Windows. To enable TLS in Windows: Open the "Control Panel" and then "Internet Options"> "Advanced" tab. At the bottom of the list, put a checkmark in front of all information, starting with "TLS." Click "OK" and reload the site.

If error 1002 persists, you should repair your Silverlight installation.

6. Problems with the order or payment

Many movies or series in Amazon Prime Video are paid - and can be borrowed and / or purchased. But what if there are difficulties with the purchase? Typical error codes can be: 2016, 2021, 2023, 2026, 2027, 2028, 2029, 2040, 2041, 2043, 2044, 2047, 2048, 2063 and 7035 .

This problem may be related to the incorrect IP assignment. Proceed as follows:

Basically: Are you perhaps not in your home country? Abroad, the Amazon Prime Video offering is severely limited due to license terms.

Tip: The next time you travel abroad, save movies and series, you might want to watch offline in the Prime Video app.

Look in your order list - there may be there to the desired purchase detailed information why the business did not come about. All information can be found at the respective purchase in the top right under "order details."

In order to borrow films or series with an Amazon account, the payment method "1-Click" must be activated.

Do you have a VPN connection if necessary? Then turn off the VPN and try again.

If necessary, change your payment method. Maybe the problem is hidden here. Changing the payment method can eliminate a hiccup during orders.

REVIEW AMAZON FIRE TV STICK 4K

A general overview of the device

Amazon fire tv stick 4k

Fire TV Stick 4K is a multimedia player that allows you to access different content, which is the equivalent of the various smart decoders produced by other well-known brands.

In addition, however, this reader allows access to some very interesting functions, such as using the Alexa voice assistant, exploiting the different potentials and products of the smart home, and other features that can turn the TV into a total control tool and also make your home smarter.

What it is and what it is used for

Fire TV Stick 4K is a multimedia player whose main objective is to transform the classic television into a smart TV, with the possibility of accessing the web through the TV and being able to take advantage of the various contents, or the applications provided by the device, which allows to radically change the concept of the classic TV.

Moreover, thanks to Fire TV Stick 4K, you can take advantage of a series of paid programs, such as Netflix and Amazon Prime, through which you have the opportunity to enjoy broadcasts, television series, and films without any particular limit.

Consequently, it is possible to compare this instrument to an entertainment system for your TV set, without having to buy a smart TV, since by connecting the player to the TV and the internet, all the various contents are accessed directly.

The main features

Let's see what the different main features of Amazon Fire Tv Stick 4K, which represents a reader for the television with many opportunities, are.

Among them stand out:

- 8 gigabytes of internal memory for installing applications, such as Infinity and various games;
- High-speed connection to the wifi network thanks to the dual antenna that allows quick

access to the network and offers a stable connection during streaming and browsing;

- Compatible with a large number of applications, both video and games;
- Quad-core 1.7 GHz which allows operations to be performed in fairly short times;
- Possibility to connect the reader via Ethernet cable, should the wifi connection not be of first quality;
- Playback of video content in 4K and Full HD, with 1080p resolution;
- Storage in the cloud of the various downloaded data, which therefore makes it possible to avoid filling the reader's memory.

These are the different functions and main features that go to distinguish this multimedia player from Amazon, thanks to which browsing online and exploiting the screen of your TV will not be a dream, but rather an operation that can be carried out without difficulty.

Smart home functions

As far as home automation is concerned, it is possible to have the opportunity to access the various devices that are connected to Alexa and the internet network.

Creating an overall connection, in fact, it is possible to have the opportunity to access home cameras: if, for example, you want to see what is happening outside your home, you can express the above command to Alexa, who connects to the cameras of your own home and at the same time make sure that the images are reproduced on television, without any inaccuracy.

Another type of function for the smart home is the control of the hob and the lights of the house, as well as other types of devices that are connected to the network and that are compatible with Alexa.

Therefore Amazon Fire TV Stick 4K allows you to have total control of the entire home, thus avoiding a series of complications that can make the situation less pleasant than expected.

Even a simple routine check can be carried out thanks to this simple reader, which allows you to have full control of your home.

Obviously, it must be remembered that all the devices must be connected to the same wifi network so that a rapid communication network can be created that is able to satisfy all one's needs.

Configuration and installation

The installation and configuration of this device is really child's play:

- Insert the device into your television
- Connect it to the power cord
- Connect to the internet using your Wifi ID and Password
- Configure the multimedia applications you need through credentials

Technical features

These are the technical features of the 4K Fire TV Stick

- Brand: Amazon
- Name: 4K Fire TV Stick
- Dimensions: 99 x 30 x 14 mm (connector excluded), 108 x 30 x 14 mm (connector included).
- Weight: 53.6 g
- Processor: 1.7 GHz Quad-core
- GPU: IMG GE8300
- Memory: 8 GB
- Connectivity Wifi : Compatible with 802.11a / b / g / n / ac Wi-Fi networks.

- Bluetooth: BT 4.2 and BLE
- Voice commands: Available with the Alexa remote control (included) or the Fire TV app, free.
- Ports: HDMI and Micro-USB (Power only)
- Audio formats: Dolby Audio, 7.1 surround sound, two-channel stereo, and HDMI audio pass-through up to 5.1.
- 4K support: Yes, HDR.
- Supported formats : Video: Dolby Vision, HDR10, HDR10 +, HLG, H.265, H.264, and VP9. Audio: AAC-LC, AC3, AC3 (Dolby Digital Plus), FLAC, MP3, PCM / Wave, Vorbis, and Dolby Atmos (EC3_JOC). Photos: JPEG, PNG, GIF, BMP
- Output resolution : 2160p, 1080p and 720p up to 60 fps
- Package Contents: 4K Fire TV Stick, HDMI extension, Alexa voice remote control (2nd generation), 2 AAA batteries, USB cable and charger, Quick start guide.

Advantages and disadvantages

Advantages:

- Compatible with all TVs;

- Easy to set up;
- Easy to use thanks to the Alexa voice assistant, which simplifies content search and access to the various Fire Stick functions.

Disadvantages:

- Slightly fragile;
- Requires a good wifi connection to work 100%;
- Sometimes the remote control cannot immediately understand the voice commands, which must be repeated again.

Conclusions and final considerations

A good multimedia player that, for those who have an old generation TV and is fully functional, represents the ideal purchase, given that this is turned into a real smart TV without having to incur high costs, given the prices that go to distinguish these appliances.

Especially recommended for those who love movies and TV series, even not recent, or for those who want to recover an episode of an old television program.

HOW TO CONTROL THE TV WITH ALEXA

How to control TV with Alexa

Compatible models

In the USA, in this regard, they are light years ahead thanks also to the Fire TV Stick that acts as a bridge and allows you to switch on the TV and control it with simple voice commands. With us, the question is a bit more complicated.

At the moment, only some TV models support the Italian version of Alexa, and everything will be more complicated until the producers release the Alexa Skills already available in the United States and the United Kingdom. You will, therefore, need to check that your TV model is among those compatible with Amazon's voice assistant and that it is marked with the Works with Alexa sticker.

Some models of Samsung, LG, and Sony (few actually) can be controlled with the Amazon voice assistant. In the case of a compatible Samsung TV, you will need to synchronize it with the SmartThings hub by downloading the app from the smart TV store and following the wizard that appears on the screen. Next, add the device to the Alexa app and start the synchronization. Same thing for Sony smart TVs: you'll need to download the TV Control Configuration app with Alexa and follow the procedure. In the end, you can adjust the volume and change channels without a remote control.

Check the TV with the Smart sockets

To turn the TV on and off with voice commands, you can connect Alexa to your TV using a smart device. Buy a intelligent socket compatible with Alexa, synchronize it with the smartphone app, and assign it a name (for example, "TV"). Just say "Alexa, turn on the TV" or "Alexa turn off the TV" to check the device.

Control TV with Alexa via Broadlink

Another possibility is given by Broadlink, an intelligent universal remote control that uses infrared technology to replicate the functions of any remote control. It is compatible with Alexa, and therefore you can manage Broadlink with voice commands (and consequently the TV).

Configure Broadlink by installing the IHC for the EU app. Once registration is complete, and the application has started, you will need to choose a product and TV model to clone remote control commands. If you can't find the brand of your TV, you can use the Learning feature of Broadlink (it detects the commands of your remote control independently).

Once you have configured the Broadlink, you will have to open the Alexa app in the Skill and Games section, type in the Broadlink search bar and activate the Broadlink Smart Home for EU skill. Detect new devices and rename the TV as you want.

From this moment on you can perform voice commands such as:

- Alexa, turn up the "Device Name" volume
- Alexa, turn up the volume by three
- Alexa, next channel
- Alexa, go to channel eight
- Alexa, turn on / off

Smart TV Samsung and Alexa

From 2019 Samsung Smart TVs will offer users more options for voice checks, using the new Bixby and AI remote control, or through Amazon Echo and Google

Home. These last two assistants will not be integrated directly on the TV but will allow simple management of TV functions, such as switching on / off, changing the channel, or raising/lowering the volume using voice commands.

Being compatible with Alexa, it is, therefore, possible to give voice commands to Broadlink itself, which in turn will transmit them to the TV. You can both use the Broadlink RM PRO +, which is equipped with both infrared and radiofrequency technology, and the Broadlink Mini 3, which is exclusively provided with infrared technology.

Furthermore, the Broadlink can be used as a complementary device to the Fire TV Stick itself.

Configuring Broadlink

In order to control the TV with Alexa with Broadlink, you will need to configure the latter and install the IHC (Intelligent Home Center) for the EU app.

After registering (better to avoid logging in from Facebook because it appears to have given problems in the past), in the app, you will have many product and brand categories to choose from to clone the commands of the corresponding remote controls.

You will then need to search for your TV brand. At this point, you'll find a sort of digital remote control on the app. Make sure it works. If you can't find the TV brand, you can take advantage of Broadlink's Learning feature, which will be able to detect commands by pressing your traditional remote control.

Activate the Broadlink skill on Alexa

After configuring the Broadlink correctly, you will need to open the Alexa app, in the Skill and Games section, type in the Broadlink search bar and activate the Broadlink Smart Home for EU skill.

Now, you will be able to access Broadlink in the Alexa app using the same credentials used before and, at this point, you will see a pop-up appear asking you to detect new devices. By clicking on the All devices icon, you should be able to view the TV.

You can rename the device however you want (this step is important because you will have to pronounce the same name in your voice commands). If you can't connect Alexa to Broadlink, make sure both are connected to the same network and that your Amazon devices are registered on Italia.

You will then be able to give your voice commands. After the first command, you can also avoid repeating the name of the device (for example, TV lounge), as Alexa will already know that you are referring to the TV.

- Alexa, raise/lower the "TV / Device Name" volume
- Alexa, raise the volume by 2
- Alexa, next channel
- Alexa, previous/next channel
- Alexa, go to channel four (44)
- Alexa, turn on / off
- Alexa silences "TV."

In case you make changes in the IHC app, to ensure proper operation, it will be better to remove the device on Alexa, search for it, and add it again.

If you want a command not recognized by Broadlink (for example, the Sky or Netflix key), you can add it by going to Scenes> Add appliance> User defined> Add and at this point press the key in question on the physical remote control so that Broadlink learns. Next, in the Alexa app, you will be able to create a routine that runs the newly created scenario on Broadlink.

How to connect Alexa to Samsung TV via SmartThings

In the USA, Alexa is perfectly compatible with SmartThings, and this allows you to control any Samsung TV that is compatible with it fully.

In Italy, the SmartThings skill exists, although at the moment, it does not fully support TVs, nor air conditioners. In most recent (and smart, of course) models, it is still possible to turn on / off the TV, raise/lower the volume, switch to the previous or next channel, or change source.

Make sure your TV supports Samsung SmartThings. The compatible models are usually the latest generation QLEDs and those that have "KS" or "KU" as the fifth or sixth digit in the code, followed by a number equal to or greater than 6.

How to check Netflix with Alexa

If, until recently, in Italy, it was impossible to control Netflix with Alexa, now it is possible with the help of Fire TV Stick.

As already mentioned in the first part of this article, the new version launched in September 2019 includes a remote control with integrated Alexa. Just press the appropriate button and ask to start a film/documentary etc. as well as browse the catalog with the item.

How to control TV (Smart and not) with Alexa and Amazon Echo?

The home assistant Amazon begins to take its first steps into the world of smart TVs and classic TVs equipped with an HDMI port. With the help of the Amazon Echo smart speakers, for example, it will be possible to change channels, increase or decrease the volume of the device, tune in to a specific channel (needless to say that pay-TV, like Netflix or Sky Go, will enjoy a march in more with super custom commands).

1. A non-smart TV with HDMI socket

If your TV is not smart, the only option to use Alexa's voice commands is to Amazon Fire TV Stick: the new generation Fire Stick (it's an HDMI dongle-type TV box) has built-in support with Alexa. The two devices communicate with each other without the slightest effort, and the range of actions that can be performed by Alexa will be such as to embarrass any skill on the market, making the legendary Amazon assistant a veritable vocal remote control ("Start Fire TV"), "See

[title] on [application]," "Show me movies with [actor]",
...).

2. Alexa and the Smart TVs

Unfortunately, using Alexa as a voice, the remote control is a process for which some basic skills are required, especially with regards to installing and managing skills. Regarding the skills of the Amazon assistant, it is also worth remembering that some skills that allow the speaker to interact with a given smart TV model are not yet present in our country. In fact, every major company operating in the Smart TV sector has its own Skill in the dedicated Amazon store. Some are already usable, others are still in progress, and in some cases, it may be necessary to use an external skill.

Connect Alexa with Bluetooth devices

The pairing of smartphones/tablets/computers with Amazon Echo via Bluetooth

Go to Bluetooth on your phone and activate the Bluetooth function (set it to "visible"). Then get close enough to Amazon Echo (over 5 meters, in my experience, it doesn't work anymore). Then you have to say "Alexa, match" and Alexa tells you to pair the phone with Amazon Echo (the name of your Echo should appear on the phone's Bluetooth menu). Amazon Echo confirms the success of the pairing with „Connection established" (connection established).

Disconnection is just as easy: " Alexa, disconnect." Anything can be reproduced via Bluetooth.

Supported Bluetooth profiles

Alexa is not able to receive phone calls or other notifications from the mobile device, nor to read text messages. Voice control is not available for Mac OS X devices (such as MacBook Air), or other Alexa enabled products. The echo does not support Bluetooth speakers that require a PIN to be entered for pairing.

Problems with Bluetooth speakers

If you have problems connecting a compatible Bluetooth speaker, you can, among other things, proceed as follows. First of all, you need to check if the speaker is on and if it is powered. Then check if there is interference (microwaves, for example, can interfere with reception).

If you can't find anything like that, you should remove the device from the Alexa app and try again. If you don't solve anything here, you should check your speaker - can it be called, for example, from your phone? If so, you should contact Amazon, because Amazon Echo seems to be the problem.

HOW TO LISTEN TO MUSIC
ON AMAZON ECHO

Can I connect my phone via Bluetooth and listen to music from my smartphone?

Echo devices are equipped with audio output with 3.5 mm cable or Bluetooth technology - yes!

How to listen to music on Amazon Echo: Alexa apps and Alexa devices like Amazon Echo and Fire TV

If you want to listen to music with Alexa and control it by voice, Alexa-App (for iOS or Android) and a device with the integrated Alexa voice assistant is enough. In general, four types of devices can be identified for this purpose:

Amazon Echo Speakers: If you have an intelligent speaker like Amazon Echo, Echo Dot, or Echo Spot, it's easier. The Alexa speakers and app are already perfectly coordinated.

Alexa speakers: third-party producers now also offer Alexa compatible speakers. In particular, Bluetooth speaker manufacturers like Bose or Sonos integrate

Alexa into their products. Below is an overview of the Alexa compatible devices.

Amazon Fire TV: music playback with Alexa also works via the TV, but only if it is connected to Amazon Fire TV. Here, the music can also be played through the music application

A special case is playing music with Alexa for subscribers of Amazon Music Prime or Amazon Music Unlimited. Voice control can also be performed via smartphone, as Amazon has already integrated the Alexa voice assistant into the Amazon music application (iOS / Android).

Smartphone: if you have installed the Amazon Music application on your smartphone, you can listen to music directly from your smartphone or stream it on an external Bluetooth speaker via your mobile phone's Bluetooth interface.

If you are thinking of listening to your music with Alexa, you will be disappointed, because Alexa can only manage the music streaming services supported by the Alexa app. In the past, music that had been converted from CDs purchased into MP3 files could be uploaded to Amazon, using the Amazon Music music streaming service. Amazon discontinued this service for new customers starting April 30, 2018. If you had an Amazon music subscription before April 30, 2018, you had to proactively select "Keep my songs" in the Amazon music settings before the end subscription.

For subscribers who have activated the "Keep my songs" option, the following restrictions apply as of April 30, as soon as the Amazon music subscription has expired:

- There is no way to reactivate Amazon Music;
- It is not possible to load other music;
- Music tracks and albums purchased on Amazon are still visible and archived for free.

Connect Amazon Alexa to YouTube and listen to YouTube videos

Since breaking between Google and Amazon at the end of 2017, Google has discontinued native support for its YouTube streaming platform for Amazon Alexa.

The reason why Google complained is that Amazon does not list Google products like Google Chromecast or Google Home in the store. This means for users of the Amazon Alexa language assistant:

The native YouTube Fire TV app no longer available

No integration of the YouTube streaming service in the Alexa app

However, it is possible to connect YouTube to Alexa via more or less complicated detours:

Alexa YouTube Skill: developer David Hacker published an unofficial Alexa YouTube skill on the GitHub programmer's website. The connection with Amazon Alexa is feasible for non-experts but complicated. The skill allows users to play the audio track of a YouTube video on an Echo speaker as a stream of music. If you want to use this solution, you need an Amazon developer account and an Amazon Web Services account.

Another way to integrate YouTube into an Amazon Alexa environment is via Fire TV. Here the video is then played back on the TV. Since Google no longer provides a native Fire TV application, Firefox and Amazon have made Internet browser applications available for Fire TV for use on YouTube. However, streaming music from the audio track to an Alexa speaker is not possible.

Listen to your favorite radio with Amazon Echo

What applies to stream music also applies to radio broadcasts: listening to the radio on Alexa and Amazon

Echo speakers is only possible if they are supported by the Alexa app. The Amazon Alexa app thus assumes the function of a barrier. TuneIn is a radio transmission service that has established itself as almost standard for radio stations around the world.

TuneIn is already available in the Alexa app as a standard selection for listening to the radio. Separate accounting is not required for use. However, TuneIn cannot be used within the Alexa app on a smartphone.

Listening to podcasts with Amazon Alexa: how to listen to podcasts with Amazon Echo

Podcasts are usually regular audio contributions on special topics, which are usually recorded by experts and then offered for streaming or as a download for later listening.

To listen to podcasts with Amazon Alexa three music streaming services are available, which Amazon Alexa supports and which can be transmitted to Alexa-enabled speakers:

- Broadcast podcasts via Alexa to Amazon Echo with Spotify Premium

- Listen to the podcasts on Amazon Kindle and Audible services with Alexa (You can try Audible here for 30 days for free on Amazon .)
- Broadcast podcasts via TuneIn to an Echo speaker

The integration of music streaming services takes place as usual through the Alexa App.

- Play and listen to audiobooks and radios with Alexa and Amazon Echo
- Various options are available for playing audiobooks and radios with Alexa and an Echo :
- Listen to audiobooks with Alexa via the Spotify Premium music streaming service;
- Listen to audiobooks via Audible on an Echo device with Alexa;
- Listen to radio programs with Amazon Music Prime or Amazon Music Prime Unlimited;
- Read Amazon's Kindle books from Alexa in Echo.

With Amazon Music Prime, radio programs are already available for streaming on an Amazon Echo speaker. However, it's necessary to have an Amazon Prime account. The same goes for Amazon Music Unlimited. Customers on Audible subscription, on the other hand, can draw on the entire range. The complete range of professional audiobooks is at your disposal.

Listen to audiobooks on Amazon devices with Alexa Kindle

If you buy an Amazon Echo speaker, you don't need to worry about the follow-up costs when using the smart speaker. With the integrated TuneIn radio service, 120,000 radio stations are ready to broadcast music for free. Enough choice to find the right offer for almost every taste in music or for podcast fans. Together with the Alexa assistance functions and the thousands of Italian radio skills, owners of an Amazon Echo speaker can listen to music for free.

However, if you like listening to music and want to compile personal playlists, you should consider signing up for an Amazon Prime subscription. For music lovers, the Amazon Music Unlimited music package offers over 5 million songs.

Alexa - voice commands for Amazon Music & similar - the most important commands

Alexa voice commands for the reproduction of certain music based on genre or popularity:

- "Alexa, play rock music."
- "Alexa, it sounds like hits from the 60s".
- "Alexa, it sounds a little jazzy."

Below are the Alexa voice commands for the reproduction of some artists. This usually requires a premium account with flat music for a music streaming service like Amazon Music Unlimited or Spotify Premium.

- "Alexa, play music of [...]
- "Alexa, play the album [...]".
- Other voice commands to which Alexa responds:
- "Alexa, what are you playing?
- "Alexa, next song."
- "Alexa, raise the volume by 10 percent".

Stop:

- "Alexa, stop."

Download music with Amazon Music Unlimited or Spotify Premium

Those who opt for the Amazon Music Unlimited or Spotify Premium music streaming service also receive the additional benefit of the music included: the songs can be downloaded to playback devices like a smartphone. Music downloads take place in offline mode. In this way, subscribers can continue to listen to their favorite music even without Internet reception, for example, when jogging or traveling by train.

Play Alexa music streaming on multiple devices

If you want to stream music via a device other than Amazon Echo, you can direct Amazon Echo's music stream to an external Bluetooth speaker. All Amazon Echo speakers are equipped with Bluetooth. The connection is simple and is carried out in three phases:

- Bluetooth speakers and Echo speakers must be connected to the same wireless network
- Press the pairing button on the Bluetooth speaker to switch to pairing mode.
- Give Alexa the voice command for pairing Bluetooth: "Alexa, colleague."

The echo will automatically connect to the Bluetooth speaker. If you want to log off again, simply give Alexa the voice command "Alexa, disconnect." Especially users of an Amazon Echo Dot can enjoy the better sound quality.

How to build a multi-room environment with Alexa and Amazon Echo

Only a few years ago, building a multi-room environment was a costly business.

With several Amazon Echo speakers, on the other hand, a multi-room system can be implemented very quickly. Here is the minimum requirement:

- At least two Amazon Echo speakers
- Amazon Music Unlimited streaming account
- Amazon Alexa App

Since all three components of the future multi-room environment are Amazon products, installation is simple:

- Clear name of the Echo speakers.
- In the Alexa app, go to the "Settings" menu and select "Multi-room music."
- Assign a user-defined group name or accept a suggestion from the Alexa app and press "Next."

- The Alexa app displays the available Amazon Echo speakers. Select it and press "Save."

The Multiroom Group was created. With the Alexa voice command "Play [Music] in [Multiroom group name]," the selected music is played on all the speakers in the group. It is important that all devices are on the same wireless network.

How to connect Audible audiobooks with Alexa

Audible offers audiobooks in various flat-rate subscriptions - if you don't want to play them via smartphone or Bluetooth speakers, but via Amazon Echo or similar, with Alexa, you'll also have the advantage of voice control.

How Alexa Audible audiobooks sound

Audible products can be easily controlled and reproduced with an intelligent Amazon Echo series speaker using a voice command without the need for skill. Whether it is cooking, ironing, or cleaning, the audiobook accompanies household tasks and can be used simply with the Alexa voice command.

To do this, the Echo device must be connected to the same Audible Amazon account, so you can start with

"Alexa, play the audiobook [title]" or "Continue my book." Those who need the daily dose of transmissions or music from the radio to fall asleep can also combine reading aloud with a timer: "Alexa, stop reading the book between [x] minutes/hours".

The most important Alexa voice commands for Audible

Listen to the audiobook: "Alexa, read QualityLand," "Alexa, read the book QualityLand," "Alexa, play the audiobook: QualityLand" or "Alexa, play QualityLand via Audible."

- Stop the audiobook: "Alexa, stop!"
- Continue to listen to the current audiobook: "Alexa, continue my book."
- Fast forward or rewind 30 seconds of the audiobook: "Alexa, rewind" or "Alexa, fast forward."
- Editing the audiobook chapters: "Alexa, next chapter" or "Alexa, previous chapter."
- Go to a specific chapter: "Alexa, go to chapter 5".
- Start a new chapter: "Alexa, start again."
- Setting or deleting the sleep timer: "Alexa, set a 30 minute / 2-hour sleep timer", "Alexa, stop

reading the book in 30 minutes / 1 hour" or "Alexa, stop the sleep timer."

- List audiobook selection: "Alexa, list my books."

Alexa: Set up the multi-room function for Amazon Echo

Put together a group of multi-room Echo speakers

Many people want 360 ° sound and intelligent multi-environment streaming, but only a few put it into practice. The reason for this is usually to be found in the high costs of a new networked system. However, it is not necessarily always the case. A multi-room system can also be assembled using Echo speakers. The biggest advantage: it costs much less than a multi-room system of an expensive brand manufacturer, it is much more compact and can also be controlled by voice.

All Amazon Echo speakers are capable of multi-room operation (Amazon)

After Amazon 's 1st generation Echo, many other variants followed each other at short intervals, innovations geared to the interests of very different users. Basically, all echoes have voice control with Alexa and the application with which they can be networked.

In this way, it is possible, for example, to create a multiple room group with the following Echo devices.

Echo devices compatible with multiple environments:

- The classic: Amazon Echo
- The compact successor: Amazon Echo 2
- Economy mini version: Amazon Echo Dot (1st and 2nd generation)
- Square speaker with display: Echo Show
- Mini round version with display: Amazon Echo Spot
- Modified version: Amazon Echo Plus

How do Amazon Echo speakers become a multiroom system?

In the Alexa App, you can group two or more Amazon Echo loudspeakers. But first, it makes sense to name the Echo devices used, which can easily be assigned later. For example, Echo Dot in the bedroom could be "bed 1". The name is important to be able to assign the luminaires clearly to the different living spaces.

How to change the name of an Echo device in just 3 steps:

First, open the Alexa app and then the main menu in the upper left corner. The main menu can be recognized by the dotted lines. Then press the "Settings" item.

Press on the name of the Echo speaker whose name you want to change.

Scroll down and select "Device Name" from the menu and press Edit. Now enter the new device name in the form field.

Set up a multiroom group in the Alexa app

Open the Alexa application and tap the overall menu, which can be recognized by the dotted lines in the upper left corner. Then select "Smart Home" from the menu.

Select "Groups" in the Smart Home menu of the Alexa application, then "Create Group."

Now select the "Multiroom music group."

Then accept the name of the preset group, or even better give the multiroom group a user-defined name. Select the devices you want to include in the group and then press "Create group."

If a multi-room group has been created, the music can now be played on all Echo devices belonging to the multi-room group. Use the following Alexa voice commands :

- "Alexa. Play music in [group name] ".
- "Alexa. Volume in [group name] 30% lower, please ".
- "Alexa. Pause music in [group name]!

If you want to play different music on multiple devices or stream multiple multi-room groups at the same time, you need to sign up for a family subscription (for example, from Amazon Music Unlimited). For example, children can listen to an audiobook in two rooms simultaneously, while their parents broadcast rock music in the living room.

These streaming services are compatible with Alexa's multi-room function

In addition to Amazon Music, there are many other popular streaming services that can be connected to Alexa. Currently, for example, the following are included:

Amazon Music / Amazon Music Unlimited (single and family subscription)

- Prime Music
- TuneIn
- Spotify (soon)
- iHeartRadio (America)
- Pandora (America)
- Sirius XM (America)
- Speaker API Connected to Alexa's Multi-Room Function

Using Spotify Connect with an Alexa multiroom group

The market leader Spotify has a particularly useful streaming feature that allows you to transfer your favorite music to one or more speakers in just two clicks. Simply start the Spotify application and click on "Available devices" at the bottom of the display. You can then select computers, speakers or tablets, and the desired multi-room group.

The only drawback is currently the limitation of each Echo speaker to a group. Unfortunately, it is not possible to assign the speakers that were already in the "kitchen" group to the "entertainment" group.

These manufacturers want to use API Connected Speaker

Amazon takes another step towards an eco-based multi-room system: the API Connected Speaker for multi-room system developers allows networked speakers to be connected to the Alexa multi-room. Voice commands like "Alexa, listen to classical music on the first floor" are then performed not only by Amazon Echo in the kitchen, with relaxing sounds, but also by the multiroom system connected in the living room. The Connected Speaker API is already available as a Developer Preview.

- Denon
- Marantz
- HEOS
- Are S
- Samsung
- Bose

AMAZON ALEXA COMMANDS

General questions

- Alexa, why is the sky blue?
- Alexa, how tall is Mount Everest?
- Alexa, what is the capital of [country]?
- Alexa, what was [artist's] the first album?
- Alexa, what is the square root of 64?
- Alexa, who is the [Band] singer?
- Alexa, how far is it from here [place]?
- Alexa, what is the definition of paradox?
- Alexa, how many kilometers are 5 miles?
- Alexa, when is the sun setting today?
- Alexa, who plays [role] in [series]?
- Alexa, what is the latest film from [Actor]?
- Alexa, when does summer time start?

Usable at any time

- Alexa, stop.
- Alexa, volume at 6. (0-10)
- Alexa, sound on.
- Alexa, repeat.
- Alexa, turn up the volume.

- Alexa, lower the volume.
- Alexa help.

Profiles

- Alexa, change the account.
- Alexa, what's the profile?

Calendar

- Alexa, when is my next date?
- Alexa, what's on my calendar?
- Alexa, what's in my calendar tomorrow at 9:00?
- Alexa, what is Saturday on my calendar?
- Alexa, add an appointment to my calendar.
- Alexa, add to my shopping calendar for Saturday 27 February at 15.00

Bluetooth devices

- Alexa, associate my device.
- Alexa, connect Bluetooth.
- Alexa combines Bluetooth.
- Alexa, disconnect Bluetooth.
- Alexa, play.
- Alexa, break.
- Alexa, back.
- Alexa, continue.

- Alexa, stop.
- Alexa, continue.
- Alexa, leave again.
- Alexa, unplug my phone/tablet.
- Alexa, connect my phone/tablet.
- Alexa, colleague.

Smart Home

- Alexa, find my devices
- Alexa, turn on the lights in the hallway.
- Alexa brings light into the living room at 20%.
- Alexa, turn on the coffee machine.
- Alexa, bring the fan to 75%.
- Alexa, turn on the external decoration.
- Alexa set the house temperature to 20 degrees.
- Alexa, lower the temperature in the bedroom.
- Alexa activates the movie timer.
- Alexa, turn on the living room.

Traffic

- Alexa, how is the traffic?
- Alexa, how am I going to work?
- Alexa, what is the traffic situation at the moment?
- Alexa, how is the traffic to [place]?

- Alexa, how is the traffic situation at [place]?

Weather

- Alexa, how's the weather?
- Alexa, will it rain tomorrow?
- Alexa, how is the weather at/in [place] this weekend?
- Alexa, how is the time in/in [place]?
- Alexa, what do weather reports say?
- Alexa, is it snowing Monday?
- Alexa, do I need an umbrella?

News

- Alexa, give me an update.
- Alexa, what's nice about the news?
- Alexa, what's new?
- Alexa, go on.
- Alexa, come back.
- Alexa, break.

Sport

- Alexa, what is the score of the [team name]?
- Alexa, how's the [Event]?
- Alexa, when does the [team] play?
- Alexa, who won?

- Alexa, who won the game [team or event]?
- Alexa, how was the match [team or event]?
- Alexa, when is the next [team] game?
- Alexa, what is the situation in the ranking of [team]?

Shopping list

- Alexa, what's on my shopping list?
- Alexa, add "butter" to the shopping list.
- Alexa, put "oil change" in my to-do list.

To sort

- Alexa, order [product].
- Alexa, buy [product].
- Alexa, I want to buy [product].
- Alexa, orders again [product].
- Alexa, add [product] to my cart. (Add a product to your shopping cart on the Amazon site)
- Alexa, track my order.
- Alexa, where is my order?

Timer

- Alexa, wake up at 6:00 in the morning.
- Alexa, set the alarm to 7:30.
- Alexa, set the weekend alarm at 9:00.

- Alexa, set a repeat alarm for Tuesday at 4:00.
- Alexa, set the timer to 10 minutes.
- Alexa, how much time is left on my timer?
- Alexa, what time is it?
- Alexa, what's the date?
- Alexa, what time is my alarm clock set?
- Alexa, reset the alarm for 7:30.
- Alexa, reset the alarm for Sunday.
- Alexa, what alarms are set for tomorrow?
- Alexa, what timers are set?
- Alexa, stop. (if the alarm or timer is sounding)
- Alexa, sleep. (if the alarm is sounding)
- Alexa, cancel the timer for 10 minutes. (if multiple timers have been set)
- Alexa, shut down in 45 minutes.

Audiobooks

- Alexa, read [title].
- Alexa, reproduce [book title].
- Alexa, play the audio book [title].
- Alexa, play [Title] on Audible.
- Alexa, break.
- Alexa, get my audiobook back.
- Alexa, go forward / backward.
- Alexa, next / previous chapter.

- Alexa, go to chapter 2.
- Alexa, leave again.
- Alexa, set a sleep timer in 30 minutes.
- Alexa, stop reading the book in 30 minutes.

Music

- Alexa, what are you playing?
- Alexa, get up.
- Alexa, refuses.
- Alexa, lower the volume.
- Alexa, turn up the volume.
- Alexa, volume at [volume level].
- Alexa, stop the music.
- Alexa, break.
- Alexa, continue.
- Alexa, next song.
- Alexa, reproduce without end.
- Alexa, set a sleep timer in 30 minutes.
- Alexa, stop the music in 30 minutes.
- Alexa, add this song (while the main music is playing).
- Alexa, I like this song (when a song or song is played from another device / radio station).

- Alexa, I don't like this song (when a song or a song is played from another device / radio station).
- Alexa, play music by [artist].
- Alexa, play [title] of [artist].
- Alexa, play my lounge playlist in random mode.
- Alexa, play new music by [Artist].
- Alexa, play [Artist].
- Alexa, play the song [title].
- Alexa, play the album [title].
- Alexa, it sounds like blues.
- Alexa, play my music randomly.
- Alexa, play music.
- Alexa, fast forwarding.
- Alexa, add the song / title to my library
- Alexa, play the playlist [Name] from Spotify
- Alexa, play the song [Name] from Spotify
- Alexa, play [music style] from Spotify
- Alexa, play songs by [artist] from Spotify

Music Search

- Alexa, what are the famous songs of [artist]?
- Alexa, listen [artist].
- Alexa, play the audio samples of [Artist].
- Alexa, search for [title] of [artist].

- Alexa, search in Prime unlimited [Title, Artist].

Radio and more

- Alexa, play a cool playback channel of [third-party music provider].
- Alexa, play the show [title].
- Alexa, plays of 'Jazz' from Spotify.
- Alexa, play the station [title].
- Alexa, play Radio One on TuneIn.

Music on Amazon Prime

- Alexa, play some top quality music.
- Alexa, listen to some top notch music to relax.
- Alexa, plays top quality music for dancing.
- Alexa, play music by [artist].
- Alexa, play the playlist [title].
- Alexa, add this song.
- Alexa, play top-quality music by [Artist].
- Alexa, plays [title] of [artist].
- Alexa, plays jazz from Prime Music.
- Alexa, play the [Name] station on Prime.
- Alexa, play the [Artist] channel on Prime.

Alexa in person

- Alexa, do you have new skills?

- Alexa, what new skills did you learn?
- Alexa, who's better? You or Siri?
- Alexa, what do you think of Apple?
- Alexa, do you have a job?
- Alexa, do you have a boyfriend?
- Alexa, do you have pets?
- Alexa, can you lie?
- Alexa, are you tired?
- Alexa, what do you do in your spare time?
- Alexa, do you know anything?
- Alexa, can you sneeze?
- Alexa, are you crazy?
- Alexa, how tall are you?
- Alexa, can you sing?
- Alexa, are you hungry?
- Alexa, can you drive?
- Alexa, are you there?
- Alexa, where are you?
- Alexa, where is your body?
- Alexa, can you swear?
- Alexa, are you beautiful?
- Alexa, who's the boss?
- Alexa, how old are you?
- Alexa, are you Skynet?

- Alexa, when is your birthday / Alexa, when are you years old?
- Alexa, when was Amazon founded?
- Alexa, do you know any poems?
- Alexa, who is your father / mother?
- Alexa, are you drinking?
- Alexa, do you use drugs?
- Alexa, tell me a joke (Chuck Norris).

Christmas

- Alexa, when is Christmas?
- Alexa, how much is missing at Christmas?
- Alexa, play a Christmas song
- Alexa, play [...]
- Alexa, do you know a Christmas song?

General phrases

- Alexa, Happy Easter.
- Alexa, test, 1, 2, 3.
- Alexa, I hate you.
- Alexa, I'm tired.
- Alexa, I'm bored.
- Alexa, I have a cold.
- Alexa, cow shit.
- Alexa, I'm coming back.

- Alexa, I'll be back again.
- Alexa, see you soon.
- Alexa, I'll see you later.
- Alexa, I'm back.
- Alexa, meal.
- Alexa, don't panic.
- Alexa, it's my birthday today!
- Alexa, I have a headache!
- Alexa, I'm drunk!
- Alexa, I have to go to the bathroom!
- Alexa, I'm sad!
- Alexa, I want to die!
- Alexa, cooking, cooking a cake ...
- Alexa, give me pleasure.
- Alexa, bye.
- Alexa, hasta view!

Other questions

- Alexa, who is the murderer?
- Alexa, where is Chuck Norris?
- Alexa, what does a cat say?
- Alexa, how's the fox?
- Alexa, will you marry me?
- Alexa, who am I?
- Alexa, did you get lost?

- Alexa, did you sleep well?
- Alexa, what should I wear today?
- Alexa, what's the use of war?
- Alexa, when the first Echo came out on the market?
- Alexa, are you kidding?
- Alexa, what's more?
- Alexa, what's going on?
- Alexa, how do you write?
- Alexa, what languages do you speak?
- Alexa, between how long does it open [company name] to [place name]?
- Alexa, when is the full moon?
- Alexa, when does the sun rise and set?
- Alexa, what planets are there?
- Alexa, do you smell this?
- Alexa, what's your job?
- Alexa, what is love?
- Alexa, do aliens exist?
- Alexa, are you Skynet?
- Alexa, when does summer come?
- Alexa, who slept in my bed?
- Alexa, who is the most beautiful of all?
- Alexa, who fired first?
- Alexa, what are the lottery numbers?

- Alexa, do you know the lottery numbers?
- Alexa, where do I live?
- Alexa, do you have a light?
- Alexa, why is the banana crooked?
- Alexa, do you want some coffee?
- Alexa, do you want a beer?
- Alexa, who is Daenerys Targaryen?
- Alexa, who is Batman?
- Alexa, who is the superman?
- Alexa, when does the time change?
- Alexa, do you know a jodel?

Various commands

- Alexa, good morning!
- Alexa, I'm about to vomit.
- Alexa, self-destructing.
- Alexa, use power.
- Alexa, sing "Happy Birthday".
- Alexa, guess what?
- Alexa, choose a card.
- Alexa, tell me a tongue twister.
- Alexa, washes dishes.
- Alexa, say something funny.
- Alexa, change profile.
- Alexa, toss a coin.

- Alexa, 99 balloons.

- Alexa, let's say the alphabet.

- Alexa, count up to [number].

- Alexa, these trinkets are cute.

- Alexa, sing 'siam tre small porcellin'.

- Alexa, repeat after me.

- Alexa, live long and in peace.

- Alexa, my armpits sweat.

- Alexa, I want a black tea. Hot.

- Alexa, make me a sandwich.

- Alexa, knock.

- Alexa, to be or not to be?

- Alexa, "hi, it's me".

- Alexa, recite me a poem.

- Alexa, do you speak Klingon?

- Alexa, play the song of death to me

- Alexa, you're fired!

- Alexa, tell me the names of the animals.

- Alexa, why is that straw?

- Alexa, I think my pig whistles!

- Alexa, BUUUUUHHHH! (very difficult)

- Alexa, surprise me.

Amazon Echo and Amazon Echo Spot - Comparison

HOW ALEXA AND DROP-IN ALEXA CALLS WORK

If there is one aspect for which Alexa devices stand out from other smart speaker management systems it is the ability to function as a message center and intercommunication between similar devices, but it is possible to do much more: the Drop In function, for example, allows you to tell everyone in the house that dinner is ready or ask to bring something from the fridge downstairs or you can send a message from the office or from the car communicating the time when you will arrive at home.

Call Alexa and Drop-In

Obviously, if you have access to Alexa's friends or family, you can communicate with them directly without having to use the phone or without having a mobile phone at home.

Finally, an "Announcements" mode is coming (available at the moment only in some countries and not in Italy) that allows the "broadcast" from one to many without the possibility of answering: the typical example is the bureau and the classes or the kitchen and all the rooms in the house.

What is Drop in, and how is it enabled?

THE Drop In mode allows you to chat from a distance

Drop in allows you to call one of the Alexa devices from your home: it can be useful to alert someone at home when you are out or it can work as an intercom between different rooms if you are lucky enough to live in so many square meters or on several floors. If you have a device with videos like Echo Spot you can do a Drop in with video.

The Drop In works basically with only the devices registered on your Alexa App, but you can expand its range by letting family and friends let you do Drop In on their devices. Even without them answering or accepting the call.

Which devices support the Drop In call?

- Amazon Echo
- Amazon Echo Dot
- Amazon Echo Show (not available in Italy)
- Amazon Echo Spot

- Amazon Echo Plus

How to start a Drop In call from your device?

The system works without problems with the devices you have at home and it is advisable that you assign a different name for each one. We have simply called the devices Alexa (our Echo plus) and Echo (our Echo Dot) as the respective activation words: at this point you will have to say "Alexa, Drop In on Echo ", your speaker will answer you twice "Echo Dot by ..., right ? "If you don't answer" Right "the Drop In call doesn't work and you hear a stop signal. If "Right" responds, two-way communication is activated with a hands-free intercom.

Obviously be careful to turn it off when necessary otherwise it becomes a "spying" system inside the house.

To stop it, simply say "Alexa, Ferma Drop In ".

How to call other homes and phones with Alexa from your home or smartphone

You can use the Drop In system as an "intercom" between two different homes with family and friends.

Drop In also works between different Alexa groups such as the home of a relative or a close friend: this must first of all be "registered" in your address book and you must allow the Alexa application to access your contacts: you can call them from Alexa with the exact name with which they appear in your address book, if you want to call them simply say "Alexa calls Tizio Caio" and if you have Echo Spot you can decide to activate or deactivate the video always with a voice command" Alexa, turn off video" or touch the screen to perform the same operation.

If you don't want to be disturbed with Drop In you can directly ask Alexa "Alexa, don't bother me" and then "Alexa, deactivate don't disturb me" to reactivate Drop in.

Call from the Alexa App

Of course you can call from your smartphone wherever you are directly on the home echo: it is a "data" call and therefore you can do it from both 3G and Wi-Fi.

Just choose Drop In from the messaging tab and click on the name that is available for calls.

Call Alexa

The Drop In function can be convenient for close relatives and friends of the heart but it could be a bit invasive in the homes of people we know less: it is sufficient that they do not authorize us for the Drop In to avoid such close relationships or temporarily activate the "non disturb "but this might not be enough.

At the same time we can always use Alexa Calls or Alexa messages from within the application or directly from the Echo.

First of all, your correspondent must have an active Alexa App or activated ECHOs.

At this point, from the contacts section of your application or simply from an Echo, all you have to do is press the name on the list and / or say "Alexa, call Tizio Caio" and a call will start waiting for the communication to open on the other side .

Attention: if our contact has the Alexa App or an Echo activated the call will be under Alexa otherwise the App will try to open the Phone app and the interface will be completely different: pay attention to it. Obviously you must have authorized the Alexa app to use the normal phone call previously.

Alexa messages

If you think a call could be a nuisance you can send both a text message (which will be converted by Alexa) and a voice message by recording it in the Alexa app itself.

Your Echo will issue a note when a new message is received and you can check it immediately or after a few minutes.

How do you check the messages received? Just ask: "Alexa, read me the messages received "the answer will be "No new message, do you want to listen to previous messages? ", Or" There are two messages for Caio Sempronio "and then he reads the messages" Test message, received at seven thirty "or" Test message 2, received right now ".

In the case of receiving a vocal message, Alexa will announce that it is a different type of message.

The messages are always available for consultation and must be deleted from the Alexa App on the smartphone.

Alexa Announcements

This mode, as mentioned, is NOT currently available in Italy but should arrive in the future and will function practically as the intercom in a single direction that is installed in schools and supermarkets: in practice the message sent by your single Echo is sent to all the other Echos of the house: you will have to say "Alexa, announce that the lunch is ready" and the message will be sent to all the Echos with no possibility of answer unless a following Drop In communication is activated.

To conclude : Alexa offers a wealth of communication options between Alexa devices and Smartphones equipped with Apps, "Open" calls, intercommunication and all through the Wi-Fi internet connection, creating new opportunities to keep in touch with relatives and friends and offering some cases (think of an elder only at home, a person with reduced mobility) the ability to communicate simply and immediately.

Alexa commands: all the questions to do to the assistant of Amazon

- Alexa, play "The Grand Tour" (by default the service will be Amazon Prime Video, Netflix is not supported)
- play music videos of Vasco Rossi (on Vevo, Youtube is not supported)
- play music / rap music / cheerful music

- play music on Spotify (if Spotify is not the default)
- put Madonna in the living room / Alexa, put Shakira in all the rooms (if you have more than one device, you can control the sound of the different rooms)
- play music to party
- play the latest Caparezza album
- reproduce that song that does "Sometimes I feel like I don't have a partner" (not yet available in Italian)
- I like this song (only on Amazon Music, to add songs to your favorites)
- add this song to my "Relax" playlist (Amazon Music only)
- what's the name of this song?
- what do you think will be the summer hit?
- open Sounds of India
- put playlist Moments of the moment on Apple Music
- follow Jovanotti on Amazon Music
- open Radio 105 (by default it will be from TuneIn but you can also download the special skill of each radio)

- read me The Little Prince / go back to the previous chapter / go to the next chapter (if you have the Audible service)
- play Night Forest / Tibetan Bells
- reproduce environmental noise rain (storm, stream, ocean, etc.)
- Alexa connect Bluetooth device / connect my phone (to connect the speaker to your smartphone via Bluetooth)

Furthermore, by connecting your calendar, you can easily manage your appointments.

- Alexa, wake me up tomorrow at 7 am / disable alarm (tomorrow's)
- wake me up at 8 with Queen's "We will rock you"
- wake me up at 6 with Radio 105 (example)
- set a recurring alarm on weekdays at 6.30am
- set the timer for 20 minutes
- set the timer for the cake for 40 minutes
- at what point is the cake timer?
- cancel the cake timer
- what time is it?
- what are the public holidays this year?

- add dinner with Luigi on May 3rd at the calendar
- what are my commitments today?
- remind me to check the oven in 10 minutes?
- what are the other reminders of today / 11th July etc.?
- how is my day tomorrow?
- what week are we in
- what am I throwing today? (thanks to the waste collection skill, you can create a calendar that reminds you of the type of waste to throw in which day)

Shopping lists and things to do

- You can create and update lists (for example, shopping or holidays) and add and remove items.
- Alexa, add to things to do "washing machine"
- what's on my to-do list?
- add "eggs" to the shopping list
- what's on my shopping list?
- remove the chocolate from the shopping list
- create the "Summer vacation" list

All skills will be part of your daily summary, which you can also customize.

Here are some of the questions to ask Alexa in this category:

- Alexa, what's the weather like today? (set the position on the Echo device)
- what's the weather like tomorrow in Viareggio?
- do i need an umbrella tomorrow?
- what's the weather tomorrow at 18?
- What is the temperature in New York now?
- what will the weather be like this weekend in Pescara?
- what is the news?
- what is my daily summary?
- how is the traffic? (you will need to have set the location and your route first)
- how is my journey to work?
- what is the result of Inter's game?
- has Milan won?
- when is Rome's next game?
- how many points does Vettel have?
- How is Roger Federer doing?

Here's what you can ask Alexa:

- Alexa, tell me the tiramisu recipe
- ask Giallo Zafferano for a quick first
- how do you make the cheesecake?
- how many calories does an ice cream have?
- where can I find vitamin B?
- what is the nearest pharmacy?
- what is the address of Banca San Paolo?
- what are the opening hours of the Ipercoop in Pomezia
- what is the phone number of the pizzeria "Da Gino"
- what is the nearest pizzeria?

Curiosities, research, mathematics and unit / currency conversions

In this category, you can really indulge yourself with the questions to ask Alexa.

You can ask Echo curiosity, mathematical calculations, historical facts and so on. If you ask Alexa about a topic, he will often read the first few lines of Wikipedia.

You can even learn English with a real course ("Alexa, open English course").

Here are some Alexa commands that you can start using:

- Alexa, why do we celebrate Republic Day?
- how many are 5 km in miles?
- how many is 3 dollars in euros?
- how many are 20 inches in centimeters?
- how much is 56 for 66?
- what does "oxymoron" mean?
- what is the definition of "litany"?
- how do you spell "everywhere"?
- Wikipedia "Humpback Whale"/ Alexa, tell me more, read on
- how old is Vasco Rossi?
- how many inhabitants does California have?
- tell me a quote from the Gladiator
- tell me more about the movie "The Great Beauty"
- what is the cast of Don Matteo
- what is the plot of the Joker movie
- where does saffron come from?
- how tall is the tallest man in the world?
- what is the hottest place in the world?
- tell me a curiosity about food
- what are the 7 wonders of the world?

- when is the next leap year
- What happened on June 28th?
- tell me a curiosity about asteroids
- what is the postal code of Spoleto
- because the sea water is salty
- when it will be spring in Peru
- what a Bitcoin is worth
- how do you say hello in Chinese
- what is Echo Show 5
- when does solar time start?
- what is the distant past of cooking
- is the panda carnivorous?
- what are the provinces of Lombardy?
- who is the President of Croatia?
- What is the population of China?
- tell me the Aquarius horoscope
- tell me the historical facts of today
- how much is a trillion to the tenth power?
- what time is the sunset?
- what's on TV tonight?
- what is the longest italian word?
- how much should I cook rice?
- what are the islands of Hawaii?
- what is the curiosity of the day?
- tell me a random number?

- what is there to see in Volterra?
- does the panda hibernate?
- who was born on August 6th?
- where is the Marmolada?
- how many books did Italo Svevo write?
- when was Uranus discovered?
- can dogs eat grapes?
- when will the next full moon be?
- tell me the story of tango
- what is the meaning of the name Riccardo?
- how much is an action of Apple?
- I have a headache, what can I do?

Shopping and e-commerce purchases

One of the advantages of Alexa and Amazon Echo is definitely the integration with the Amazon ecosystem.

So, if for media the immediate integration takes place with services and products like Amazon Music and Audible, it is obvious that shopping on the Amazon platform is the most natural activity you can do.

Thanks to the skills of third parties, it will then be possible to complete purchases on other platforms, even if this category is still very limited (it is possible, for example, to order previously ordered food from JustEat).

Regarding purchases on amazon.it, at the moment it is possible to ask Alexa for information on the catalog, add certain products and ask questions about the status of orders already made.

- Alexa, order / buy coffee (at this point, he will look for coffee in the catalog and suggest a product)
- add it to the cart
- track my last Amazon order / where my order is (Alexa add face cream to my cart
- what are today's offers?

Fun and pastimes: the questions to ask Alexa

- Alexa, sing a rap song
- tell me a joke
- what is the meaning of life?
- when will i die?
- how are you?
- who is your father?
- will you marry me?
- plays the guitar
- tell me a ridge

- give me an Easter egg on the cinema
- how does the lion?
- tell me a story
- tells the Ugly Anattracolo
- what is your favorite superhero
- open Question of the day
- tell me a joke about Pierino
- open this or that
- tell me a cold
- tell me a tongue twister
- give me a riddle
- do beatbox
- make the wind noise
- tell me a proverb
- tells a fairy tale

Messages, calls and drop-ins with Alexa

- Alexa, make a call
- Alexa, call "device name"
- Alexa, send a message
- Alexa, answer the call
- Alexa, hang up
- Alexa, reproduce my messages
- Alexa activates / deactivates video (with Amazon Echo Show or Spot)

- Alexa, drop-in
- Alexa, Skype mom / call mom on Skype
- Alexa, announces that he is ready at the table
- Alexa, do not disturb (when you do not want to receive calls or messages)